'Round the world cooking library
French Cooking

A modern collection of simple regional cooking

Recipe and photo contributions
by the French gourmet magazine
'La Bonne Cuisine,' Paris

DAVID & CHARLES : NEWTON ABBOT

Contents

0 7153 6240 2

Produced by Plenary Publications International, Inc., New York, Amsterdam Office, in the Netherlands for David & Charles (Holdings) Limited South Devon House – Newton Abbot – Devon

Cup measures in this book are based on an eight ounce cup.

La France à table

To most people the pleasures of really good food and wine are an occasional reward in a busy life. To the French, they are pleasures that really belong to daily life. Eating and drinking in France is the expression of an ancient tradition, refined over the centuries. It is a central pillar of family and social life and a serious occupation for which Frenchmen allow themselves plenty of time. It is true that more and more snack bars are beginning to appear in the cities and that along the highways and turnpikes more roadside restaurants are being built where you can eat a quick meal that has cost no great pains to prepare. But in the provinces, eating is still what it has been for centuries in France: a sacred ritual performed with single-minded concentration and deep satisfaction. If you are invited to lunch by a Frenchman who lives out in the provinces, you can plan to remain at the table from half past twelve until at least four o'clock. Not only do you savor the food and wine, but the whole meal, from beginning to end, is designed as an affable and special occasion. You arise from the table, mellowed a little by the wine, at peace with life and far from your troubles.

Sunday is an important day in France. It is the day when the city dweller, who works far away from home during the week and has to content himself with a quick bite to eat at the local bistro, takes his family out to participate in the national pastime of good eating. This is the main reason for Sunday's great exodus of cars from the cities, packed with father, mother, the small children, grown children and grandparents, whenever possible. Their destination is a restaurant in the country where the cook and the wine cellar have acquired a good reputation for dependability. In any country restaurant where there is a cook who takes his art seriously, Sunday is the climactic achievement of a week's efforts. You can be sure that the restaurant will be filled right down to the last table and that the cook has carefully ordered the exact quantity of fresh fish, vegetables, meat, game and fruit that is needed. There is usually only one meal on the menu, but it is worked out to the finest detail.

Most of the restaurants do not even give you a written menu on Sunday, you just sit down and wait for whatever comes. The large room which remains closed during the week is now opened to accommodate the patrons. It has fresh flowers arranged by Madam herself, and there is extra help brought in from the village. At about twelve o'clock the room begins to fill up and by one o'clock every seat is taken; the door is then locked, a sign reading 'full'

4

Even in small wayside restaurants truck drivers enjoy such specialties as escargots.

Vegetable market in the Périgord.

is hung outside and the party begins. Though the sole entertainment is to be food and conversation, no one will leave until the black coffee and brandy have arrived to mark the end of the meal, some three and a half hours later. The main dish of these Sunday meals is usually chicken, a choice that would have gladdened the heart of Henry IV, King of France from 1589–1610. His great ideal was for every Frenchman to have a chicken in the pot on Sunday an unimaginable social and economic achievement for those times. But even if all of France were to eat chicken on Sunday, it would certainly not mean that everyone ate chicken prepared in the same way, which would be even more unimaginable. From region to region chicken differs in color, taste, fragrance and aroma, character, sauce, garnishing and stuffing. You could travel throughout France for a year, or perhaps two, and eat a chicken prepared in a totally different way each Sunday.

This is one of the most enchanting aspects of French cooking: that it is actually a collection of regional dishes and cooking ideas, each one totally different in character. All the great French chefs look to all the different regional cuisines for their inspiration. Alexandre Dumaine, one of the greatest French cooks of the last century, once confessed that when he felt that his inspiration was drying up he would go to spend a few days with his old aunts in the country. There were always a few new and exciting ideas in their kitchen.

The word chauvinist originated in France, and few Frenchmen can be persuaded to forsake their beautiful country. But France is an enormously varied country for its size and every Frenchman is convinced of the evident superiority of the food and wine of his own region. You can certainly recognize the cooking by the region from which it comes. Normandy, in the northwest of France, is a region of lush green fields where fat cattle graze. It is covered with great apple orchards filled with soft pink blossoms in spring. As you might expect from all this, Normandy cooking features tender veal, sauces made of thick cream and golden yellow butter. It is scented with the fresh aroma of Calvados, a potent spirit distilled from apple cider. Dessert here is often a delicious apple pie. The cheese of the region is piquant.

Brittany, on the other hand, is a relatively poor province. The indifferent soil is covered with a

Crab fishing in Britanny. On Sundays the whole family goes out into the country to enjoy regional cooking on the terraces of the small restaurants.

growth of tangled weeds. There are barren plains, rocky uplands and fir woods swept by strong winds that blow off the ocean. Ever since man can remember, the Bretons have sought their livelihood from the ocean. The whole of Britany seems to give off the odor of silver oysters and mussels, of lobsters and shrimps, of seaweed and fish. Seafood is usually eaten fresh from the fisherman's nets, prepared as simply as possible without complicated sauces and garnishings. Here you can eat fishsoups and crêpes (thin pancakes) prepared from buckwheat. Thanks to the soft humid seawind, in early spring the finest vegetables grow in Brittany's sheltered gardens. Brittany produces France's best asparagus, cauliflower and artichokes.

The southwest of France is a culinary paradise. In this region of the Périgord you can go for days and days without ever encountering a bad restaurant. Every real chef seems to have a streak of genius and every housewife is a remarkably good cook. The Périgord is the land of geese. In November these geese find their destiny in large brown earthenware pots, where they remain the whole winter to age in their own fat, called 'confit'. The Périgord is also the land of the fabulous truffles, sometimes called 'black diamonds'. These are mysterious, black, button-capped fungi which grow

underground in the shade of oak trees. When these marvellous fungi ripen in November they are found by old experienced country women who walk in the open fields leading a pig on a line and carrying a basket filled with ears of corn. Pigs are mad about truffles and sniff them out with unerring accuracy from their shady beds. The pig roots for them in the ground, but just as it gets ready to bite into the delicious fungi, the old woman quickly sticks an ear of corn in its mouth and grabs the truffle for herself. She lets the truffles stand for one day in a basket with eggs, which serve the purpose of absorbing some of the penetrating odor.

On the following day she sells the truffles at the market in Sarlet, where she can usually get at least £17 a pound. The Périgord is also the home of the finest pâté, made from expensive goose liver and truffles, and produces fine duck liver, turkey, veal, pork and chicken seasoned with chopped truffles and brandy. No wonder that all the European kingdoms and principalities of the 18th and 19th century wanted a cook from the Périgord!

As we near the snow-covered chain of the Pyrenees in the south, the cooking becomes more piquant and spicy. The Spanish and Basque temperaments are evident in the preparation of the chicken and in omelets and the sausages

made with tomatoes and peppers. A good Basque fish soup should be lively and pungent enough to make the hair on your head stand on end. South of the Central Massif of Auvergne, lies the Languedoc. This land was the cradle of French civilization. It produced the first distinctive French literature and music as far back as the 11th century. The glorious contribution of this region to France's great cuisine is the 'cassoulet', a stew of white beans, goose or chicken, pork, bacon and many fine herbs. The 'cassoulet' has become almost a national tradition for all of France. Though it began as a humble dish, it has made its way to the Champs Elysées. The story is told that a shoemaker who lived in one of the small villages of the Languedoc called Castelnaudary, would close his shop every Thursday and put up a sign over the door which read 'closed for reasons of cassoulet.' Moving farther east, we come into lovely Provence, where the sun shines with the same generosity as it does in Italy. The hills give off the odor of the herbs that have been used to enrich the cooking in the area ever since people can remember: basil and thyme, marjoram and rosemary, fennel and anise. Little wonder that all these herbs find a place for themselves in any number of Provençal dishes, for example in the famous 'bouillabaisse' from

Marseille, which is believed to have originated from a Greek recipe (the Greeks ruled over Marseille in 600 B.C.), and in the leg of lamb and the chicken as well as the charcoal grilled fish, the ratatouille or any of the colorful summer vegetable dishes.

Provençe is also a land of olive trees with knotty trunks and silver leaves. In the troubled Mediterranean world of old, olive trees were a symbol of peace since it took them twenty years to bear fruit and it only made sense to plant them in a land of peace. Provençe is also the land of garlic. The Provençals make a sauce of garlic and olive oil which they call 'aioli.' It may, in fact, be the oldest sauce on earth. The Phoenicians sailed the Mediterranean Sea in narrow boats many centuries before King Solomon was born. They took jars and vats of this sauce with them on their journeys and ate it with the fish they caught. The Phoenicians, like many other people around the Mediterranean (and some modern health food advocates) ascribed considerable powers to garlic. They thought it provided stamina and combatted infection and disease.

From Provençe's hot sun we move to the snow-covered tops of the French Alps that rise to a height of more than 14,000 feet. The economy of mountain regions is of necessity somewhat

spartan. The people eat what the mountains and hills can produce, mainly potatoes and milk and cheese from the cows that graze in Alpine meadows. Not surprising, then, that the most characteristic dishes of the French Alps consist of potatoes, milk, cream and cheese. But these dishes are prepared with true French taste and feel for the right blend of ingredients. 'Gratin Dauphinois' (Potatoes au Gratin Alpine style) is a simple Alpine dish that is fit for a king!

Traveling north through the Rhône valley we arrive at Lyon, the gastronomical stronghold of France. Lyon is a city where it is impossible to eat mediocre food. Here you find the really great

chefs and the famous 'mères,' a dedicated breed of ageing ladies who run small restaurants and do the cooking themselves. The whole region is famous for its cooking, and in Lyon it is especially good. You can eat the best chicken in the world, prepared with a cream sauce, or eggs and truffles, or the whitest of frog legs from the swamps of Bresse, a bare 35 miles away. You can eat the best beef or the most tender ham prepared in white wine and smothered in hay, or trout out of the mountain streams of the Cévennes prepared in a sauce made from crayfish from the brooks of the neighboring Jura, or pike perch fished from Lake Geneva.

Still farther north, we come into the historic province of Burgundy, where each dish is mellowed with a sauce prepared with fragrant Burgundy wine. In Burgundy almost everything is brilliantly cooked in red and white wine: not only chicken, but also eel and even eggs are poached in a wine sauce. After a rain you can find the thick Roman snails that are such a delight to eat. The snails are cleaned and put back into their shells, which are then stuffed with a stiff sauce of butter, garlic and parsley, and baked. This is also the land of exuberant wine festivals centered on the vaulted winecellars of historic cloisters and abbeys where people feast in the grand old style of the Middle Ages. Burgundy is an area where wine is a food, a tradition and a way of life. The Hotel Terminus in Dijon supplies its rooms with three taps: one for hot water, one for cold, and one for wine. We end our gastronomic travels through France in Alsace, the area right by the German border. Here the cooking combines the substantial quality of German food with the refinement of French cooking. You can eat the best cauliflower in the world, the finest sausages and priceless fruit pies and tarts. The secret of great French cooking lies in two things. The first is, as it must be, the good quality of the raw materials. There are no housewives in the world more difficult or critical than the French when it comes to buying food.

French bakers must knead fresh bread at least twice a day to satisfy the Frenchman's craving for crisp loaves tasting exactly as bread should. Even in the smallest inland villages you can get fresh fish. The French are never happier than when they can go into the country to buy fresh first quality butter, eggs, cheese, vegetables, fruit and honey.

The second part of the secret of good cooking is patience. If it concerns eating and drinking, a Frenchman is never in a hurry. He is always ready to wait for absolute perfection. He is patient enough to raise livestock and game until it is exactly right. He is patient enough to age cheese slowly until it reaches the perfect degree of piquancy. He is patient enough to leave the wine in the cellar until it reaches its peak. He has the patience to simmer a sauce until all the flavor and aroma have blended just enough, or to watch a meat dish slowly reach perfection over the lowest heat for hours. This exemplary patience comes from the Frenchman's great respect for food. There is the story of an old French marquis who stood beside a basket of pears in his room. He carefully picked up each pear, tenderly examined it and then replaced it in the basket. Finally he chose just the pear he wanted and then called his butler: 'Jacques,' he said, 'wake me up tonight at precisely twelve minutes after three. Just at that moment this pear will have reached the perfect degree of ripeness and that is the moment I should like to eat it.'

Cheese.

In a moment of almost serious despair, President de Gaulle once said: 'How is it possible for people to govern themselves in a land where there are more than 400 different kinds of cheeses.' Cheese is an important part of any hot meal in France and a Frenchman eats two hot meals each day. Cheese is served after the main course and before the dessert or fruit. Sometimes the cheese course is only a pretext for another glass of the wine that has been served with the main course. Cheese and wine make a perfect gastronomic combination: 'a happy marriage' as the French say. Many French cheeses have an ancient history. Take Roquefort, for example. This is the blue streaked sheep's cheese which comes out of the barren highlands of Rouergue. In this very poor area where the ground is rocky and hardly anything grows except rye, people have been making sheep's cheese since prehistoric times. According to legend, there was once a young shepherd who sat in one of the deep caves eating Roquefort cheese with rye bread. Evidently he went off and left some of his cheese and bread lying in the cave. Upon his return, three weeks later, he was surprised to find that the cheese now had blue-green streaks. The shepherd did not know it then, but the streaks came from a mold called Penicillium (the same mold from which penicillin comes) and these streaks were produced when spores from the moldy rye came in contact with the cheese. But he did know that it tasted fragrant and delicious. That was about two thousand years ago and ever since then the inhabitants of this poor valley have left this sheep's cheese in the caves of Roquefort to ripen and produce the mold.

Soft pungent Camembert cheese comes from Normandy. It was created around 1791 by an industrious country woman, Madame Harel. She is reputed to have received two statues and a kiss from Napoleon for her discovery. From the French Jura come Gruyère cheeses with their fine nutty aroma. These cheeses are ideal for 'au gratin' dishes because of their even taste and aroma. The green heart of France, the area surrounding the Loire river, produces the soft, sour, white goat cheeses. The French Alps produce their own luxurious creamy cheeses like Reblochon; Provence produces goat cheeses which are seasoned with the aromatic Provençal herbs.

Wine.

In the sixteenth century there was a French king who, of all his handsome titles, preferred to be known as 'King of France and Lord of the best vineyards in the world.' The title may have been slightly presumptuous, but no one would argue with its accuracy.

France has the best vineyards in the world. Nowhere on earth are so many great wines produced in such a small area. The reason for this lies in a happy combination of circumstances. The French climate is predominately cool; spring is humid, summers are moderate and the autumn is long and sunny. French soil is rocky and loose, it retains warmth but does not hold water. And not least, the French wine growers and vintners have an inborn feel for balance and harmony, they have faultless good taste and a deep love for wine.

In the low billowing hills of the north are the Champagne vineyards. This is a delicate white wine which is bottled not more than four months after it has been pressed. It is then put in deep mile-long cellars which lie under the chalk-cliff vineyards. By a natural process, a second fermentation takes place in the wine and carbon dioxide is formed. The bottles are specially corked and reinforced with wire so that the gas cannot escape and remains

8

in the wine. When the wire is loosened and the cork is skillfully pried off, releasing a cool flow of this festive wine, it bubbles out into the glass and you can enjoy 'the smile of France' as it is called.

More than a thousand years ago, monks laid out the vineyards for Burgundy wines on the slopes of a chain of hills overlooking the eastern border of France, the Côte d'Or. They chose the spot on which to plant grapevines by tasting the soil. Obviously this method had a great deal to recommend it since the best wines of Burgundy are still those grown on the grounds chosen by the monks. Red Burgundy wines are luxurious and full-bodied, they are velvety in color and may have a faint odor of violets or cinnamon, or of raspberries and blackberries. White Burgundy wines, which look slightly greenish-gold in the bottle, are dry and subtle with a distinctive bouquet and a nutty taste.

From around the western port city of Bordeaux come the fine Bordeaux wines. There are more than 10,000 'châteaux' (small castles) in this area of gently rolling hills. Most of France's greatest wines bear the names of one of Bordeaux' seventeen districts, and of the many wines bottled in the châteaux, the best are labelled *crus classés*. The great wine districts of Bordeaux, each with its characteristic soil, surround the city like a wreath.

Wine cellar master from Bordeaux. Grape-picking along the Rhône and in the Elzas. The mule is a typical sight for the wine regions around the Rhône, and so are the deep baskets of the Elzas vineyards.

Médoc, one of the best known, produces a strongly flavored, light and aristocratic red wine. Graves makes a pleasant soft white wine and a robust red wine. Sauternes produces amber colored, honey-sweet white wines with a flower fragrance. Saint Emilion has full-bodied, masculine, dark red wines. Pomerol, Bourg and Blaye all have dark sparkling, full-bodied red wines.

In Eastern France, close by the German border in Alsace, there are vineyards that produce wines with the odor of spring blossoms. These Alsatian wines are light and fruity and are sometimes called 'the young girls' by the French. From the area around the Rhône, where the sun has a southern glow, comes the robust and herb-scented Côtes du Rhône, with its deep-red color.

From the area around the Loire, France's most beautiful and poetic river, where the French Kings of the Renaissance built castles for their wives and mistresses, come a group of lovely white wines and the pleasant rosés which supposedly cooled the bad temper of Josephine de Beauharnais, Napoleon's first wife.

In France, wine drinking is an art, and like any art it has certain rules which must be followed. There is nothing difficult or mysterious about how to use wine properly for the table. The rules to follow are all

simple and based on common sense, but they can add a great deal of pleasure to wine drinking and can make any wine yield its best qualities.

Wine temperature.

Generally red wines are served at room temperature and white wines are served at cellar temperature. Room temperature is about 60°–64°F. You bring the wine to this temperature by leaving the bottle all day in a room where the temperature is not more than 70°F. Only simple, cheap and young red wines, that do not have a great deal of character, are drunk cooled.

White wines are usually drunk at cellar temperature, about 50°–54°F. A good white wine which is too cold loses its bouquet and taste. Only very sweet and sparkling wines are chilled. But they are never chilled to less than 43°F. (Sparkling wines that are too cold will not fizz.) Never put ice cubes in wine. This makes the wine very thin and it loses both its taste and bouquet. Wine should never be treated or drunk like a soft drink!

Which wine first?

If you intend to serve several wines during the course of a single meal, always drink white before red, light before strong, dry before sweet and cheap before expensive. That way you can always get the best value from your wine.

Combinations.

With fish, shellfish and cold vegetable dishes you should drink white wine or dry sparkling wine. With meat dishes and cheese, drink dry red wine. With desserts, fruit, ice cream etc. drink sweet white wine or sweet sparkling wine (demi-sec).

Rosé can be drunk with either fish or meat, game and fowl.

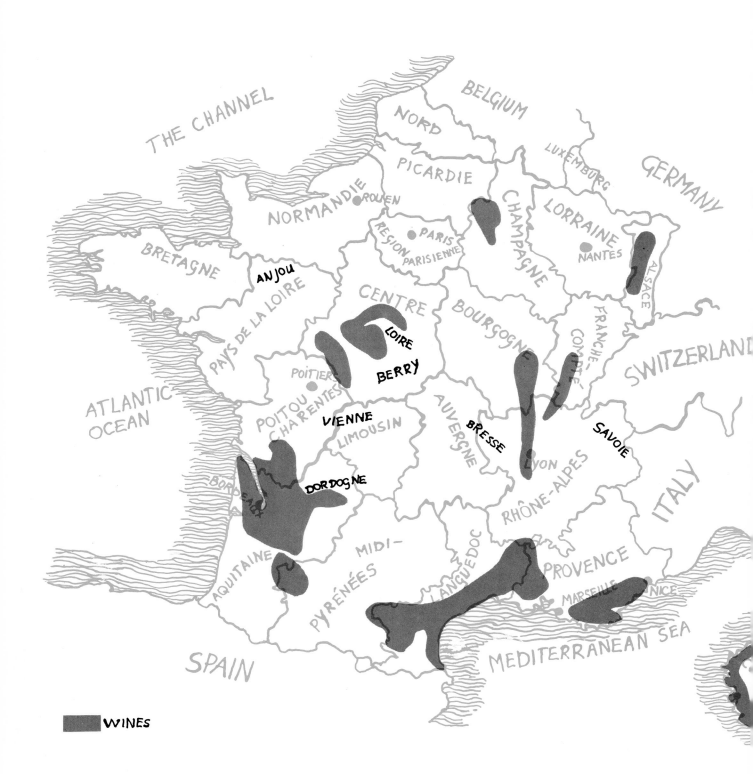

THE CHANNEL

BELGIUM

NORD

PICARDIE

LUXEMBURG

GERMANY

CHAMPAGNE

LORRAINE

NORMANDIE

ROUEN

RÉGION PARISIENNE

PARIS

ALSACE

BRETAGNE

ANJOU

CENTRE

BOURGOGNE

FRANCHE-COMTÉ

NANTES

SWITZERLAND

PAYS DE LA LOIRE

LOIRE

POITIERS

BERRY

ATLANTIC OCEAN

POITOU-CHARENTES

VIENNE

LIMOUSIN

AUVERGNE

BRESSE

SAVOIE

LYON

ITALY

DORDOGNE

BORDEAUX

RHÔNE-ALPES

AQUITAINE

MIDI-PYRÉNÉES

LANGUEDOC

PROVENCE

MARSEILLE

NICE

SPAIN

MEDITERRANEAN SEA

WINES

Cheeses

Paris and surroundings
Brie
Coulommiers
Saint-Paulin

Northern France and Champagne
Maroilles
Caprice des Dieux

Alsace
Carré de l'Est
Munster

Normandie
Camembert
Monsieur
Neufchâtel
Pont l'Evêque
Boursin
Demi-Suisse
Livarot

Bretagne
Port du Salut
Saint-Paulin
Le Roi

Anjou and Poitou
La Hippe
Saint-Maure
Saint-Paulin
Cremet

Berry
Valençay
Crottin de Chavignol

Bourgogne
Epoisses

Bresse
Bresse Bleu

Franche-Comté
Gruyère
Comté

Savoie
Reblochon
Tomme de Savoie
Tomme au marc de raisin

Provence
Banon
Poivre d'Ane
Tomme d'Arles

Auvergne
Roquefort
Bleu des Causses
Cantal
Saint-Nectaire
Bleu d'Auvergne

Wines

Dordogne
Monbazillac
Bergerac
Parchément

Bordeaux
Médoc (Margaux, St. Julien,
Pauillac, St. Estèphe)
Graves
Sauternes
Côtes de Bordeaux
Entre deux Mers
St. Emilion
Pomerol
Côte de Fronsac
Côte de Bourg
Côte de Blaye

Loire
Pouilly Fumé
Sancerre
Vouvray
Bourgueil
Saumur
Anjou
Muscadet

Champagne
Champagne
Bouzy

Alsace
Riesling
Sylvaner
Pinot
Gewürztraminer
Tokay
Muscat

Bourgogne
Chablis
Côte de Nuits (Nuits-St.
Georges, Gevrey-Chambertin,
Vosne-Romanée,

Chabolle-Musigny)
Côte de Beaune (Pommard,
Volnay, Meursault,
Puligny-Montrachet,
Aloxe-Corton)
Mâconnais (Pouilly-Fuissé)
Châlonnais (Mercurey, Rully,
Givry)
Beaujolais (Fleurie, Juliénas, St.
Amour, Chiroubles, Morgon,
Brouilly)

Côtes du Rhône
(Côte Rôtie, Hermitage,
Chateauneuf-du-Pape, Tavel,
Gigondas)

Franche Comté
Arbois
Château Châlon

Provence
Côtes de Provence
Cassis

Languedoc-Roussillon
Blanquette de Limoux
Banyuls
Muscat de Frontignan

Hors d'oeuvres

Quiche au jambon

Ham quiche

6 servings

Pastry:
1½ cups sifted all purpose flour
½ teaspoon salt
½ cup butter, cut into small
     pieces
1 egg yolk
3 tablespoons cold water

Filling:
½ pound boiled ham, cut into
     small pieces
¼ pound Swiss cheese, grated
4 eggs
1 tablespoon flour
1 cup milk
½ cup heavy cream
¼ teaspoon salt
     Freshly ground black pepper
3 tablespoons butter, melted

Sift the flour with the salt into
a bowl. With a pastry blender
or the fingertips, blend the
butter into the flour. Stir in the
egg yolk and water. Form the
pastry into a ball. Wrap in wax
paper and chill for 30 minutes.
Knead the pastry on a lightly
floured board for 2 minutes.
Roll and fit the pastry into a
9 inch pie plate. Add diced ham
and grated cheese to the
uncooked pastry shell.
Combine eggs, flour, milk,
cream, salt and pepper. Pour
over the ham and cheese.
Add melted butter. Bake in a
400° oven for 30 minutes.

Pipérade Basquaise

Eggs in the style of the Basque country

4 servings

2½ tablespoons olive oil or
      vegetable oil
4 scallions, finely chopped
2 cloves garlic, crushed
2 green peppers, cut into strips
3 medium sized tomatoes,
     peeled, seeded and chopped
¼ teaspoon salt
     Freshly ground black pepper
¼ teaspoon thyme
1 bay leaf
3 tablespoons butter
4 slices lean bacon
8 eggs

Heat the oil in a skillet.
Sauté scallions and garlic for
two minutes. Add peppers and
continue cooking for three
minutes. Add tomatoes, and
season with salt and pepper.
Add thyme and bay leaf.
Simmer uncovered for 15
minutes stirring occasionally.
Fry bacon in one tablespoon
butter until lightly browned on
both sides. Season eggs with
salt and pepper. Scramble eggs
in remaining 2 tablespoons
butter. Place the eggs on a hot
serving plate. Make a trough
down the centre. Fill trough
with vegetables. Arrange bacon
round the sides of the dish.

Coquilles St. Jacques provençale

Scallops with tomato and garlic

4 servings

- 1 pound scallops
- ¼ cup all purpose flour
- 1½ tablespoons butter
- 2 medium sized tomatoes, peeled, seeded and chopped
- 2 cloves garlic, crushed
- 2 tablespoons finely chopped parsley
- ¼ teaspoon salt
  Freshly ground black pepper
  Tomato sauce

Dredge the scallops in flour. Heat the butter in a frying pan and brown scallops for three minutes over moderately high heat. Add tomatoes, garlic and parsley. Season with salt and pepper. Stir carefully and simmer over low heat for 10 minutes. Serve very hot on scallop shells or small dishes topped with tomato sauce.

14

Salade Niçoise

Salad Riviera style

4 servings

- 8 *large lettuce leaves*
- 2 *hard boiled eggs, quartered*
- 2 *medium sized ripe tomatoes, cut into wedges*
- 8 *canned anchovy fillets*
- 8 *black pitted olives, halved*
- 1 *(6 ounce) can tuna, flaked into large pieces*
- 1 *green pepper, cut in half and then into strips*
- 2 *teaspoons capers*

For the dressing:

- 1½ *tablespoons olive oil or vegetable oil*
- 1½ *teaspoons tarragon vinegar*
- ½ *teaspoon salt*
  Freshly ground black pepper
- 1 *clove garlic, crushed*

Simmer green pepper in boiling water for 5 minutes and rinse in cold water. Wash the lettuce leaves and dry with paper towels. Place the lettuce leaves in a salad bowl and arrange all the remaining ingredients on top. Combine olive oil, vinegar, salt, pepper and garlic. Toss the salad with the dressing just before serving.

Gougère

Cheese puff

6 servings

- 1 *cup milk*
- 4 *tablespoons butter, cut into small pieces*
- ½ *teaspoon salt*
  Freshly ground black pepper
- 1 *cup sifted all purpose flour*
- 4 *eggs*
- 1 *cup Swiss cheese, grated*
- 2 *tablespoons milk*

Place the milk, butter, salt and pepper in a saucepan. Bring milk to boiling point, adjusting the heat so the butter has completely melted when the milk boils. Remove the pan from the heat and add the flour all at once. Stir the flour into the milk vigorously and place the pan over a moderate heat. Cook for two minutes until the dough can be formed into a ball and there is a film of flour on the bottom of the pan. Remove the pan from the heat and add the eggs one at a time, beating each egg well into the mixture before adding the next egg. Reserve ¼ cup of cheese. Beat remaining cheese into the dough. Butter and flour a cookie sheet. Draw a 9 inch circle in the flour. With a soup spoon, place balls of dough around the circle so that the balls are just touching each other. They will run together as they bake. Brush with milk and sprinkle with remaining cheese. Bake in a 375° oven for 40 minutes. Remove from the oven and cool on a wire rack before breaking into pieces. In Burgundy this pastry is considered the ideal accompaniment to a glass of wine. It can also be served with a salad instead of bread, or the center may be filled with either meat, chicken or fish prepared in a sauce. The Gougère freezes very successfully.

Tarte à l'oignon

Onion pie

4 servings

Pastry:

- 1 *cup sifted all purpose flour*
- ¼ *teaspoon salt*
- ¼ *cup butter cut into small pieces*
- 1 *egg*
- 2 *tablespoons cold water*

Filling:

- 3 *tablespoons butter or margarine*
- 6 *medium sized yellow onions, cut into thin rings*
- ¼ *teaspoon salt*
  Freshly ground black pepper
  Dash nutmeg
- 3 *egg yolks*
- ⅔ *cup heavy cream*

Measure flour into a bowl. Add salt. Combine butter with the flour using a pastry blender or fingertips. Add egg and water. Stir with a fork, and form pastry into a ball. Wrap in wax paper and chill for one hour. Roll out the pastry and fit it into an 8 inch pie plate, flan ring or quiche tin. Fry onions in hot butter over moderate heat. Cover skillet and simmer onions for 30 minutes, stirring occasionally. Season onions with salt, pepper and nutmeg. Combine egg yolks and cream with a fork and add to the onions. Remove from the heat and fill into pastry shell. Bake in a 400° oven for 30 minutes. Serve hot.

Pissaladière

Onion and tomato pie

4 servings

Pastry:
- ½ *package (1¼ teaspoons) dry yeast*
- 2 *tablespoons lukewarm water*
- 1¼ *cups sifted all purpose flour*
- ¼ *teaspoon salt*
- 2 *tablespoons cold butter cut into small pieces*
- 1 *egg*

Filling:
- 3 *tablespoons olive oil or vegetable oil*
- 6 *medium sized onions, cut into thin rings*
- 2 *cloves garlic, crushed*
- 2 *medium sized tomatoes, peeled, seeded and chopped*
- ¼ *teaspoon oregano*
- ¼ *teaspoon salt*
- *Freshly ground black pepper*
- 1 *(2 ounce) can anchovy fillets*
- 12 *black olives, pitted*

Dissolve yeast in water and allow to stand for 10 minutes. Sift flour into a bowl. Add the salt. Blend the butter into the flour with a pastry blender or fingertips. Add egg and cold water. Stir with a fork and form into a ball. Knead lightly for one minute. Place pastry in a bowl. Cover with a towel and leave for two hours. The dough will rise slightly. Knead dough for two minutes until smooth. Roll out dough on a floured board and fit into an eight inch pie plate, flan ring or quiche pan. In the meantime, heat oil in a skillet. Add onions and garlic. Cover and simmer for 15 minutes, stirring occasionally. Add tomatoes and oregano. Season with salt and pepper and simmer uncovered for 15 more minutes until all the liquid has boiled away. Fill onions and tomatoes into the pie shell. Bake 30 minutes in a 375° oven. Decorate baked pissaladière with anchovies arranged in a crisscross design. Place halved olives in the spaces between anchovies. Serve hot.

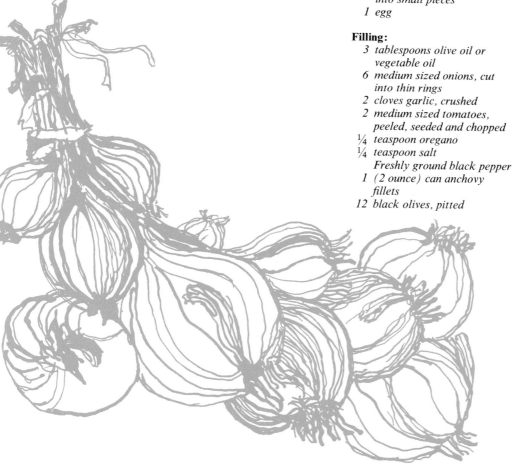

Croustade aux fruits de mer

Fruits of the sea in pastry

8 servings

    2 packages frozen puff
      pastry or 1 prepared
      pie shell
    1 egg, lightly beaten

Filling:

    1 cup dry white wine
    ½ cup water
    ½ cup clam broth (from
      canned clams)
    1 small yellow onion, cut
      into thin slices
    1 slice lemon
    1 pound flounder fillets
    ½ pound scallops
    12 medium sized shrimp
      Freshly ground black pepper
      to taste
    1 (5 ounce) can whole
      baby clams
    ¼ pound mushrooms, finely
      chopped
    1 tablespoon butter
    1 teaspoon lemon juice

Sauce:

    1½ tablespoons butter
    1½ tablespoons flour
    1 tablespoon parsley,
      finely chopped
    2 egg yolks
    ¼ cup heavy cream

Thaw the pastry and form into 2 balls. Knead on a floured board for one minute. Roll out two circles of puff pastry, one about 12 inches in diameter and the other about 9 inches. (Cut circles using dinner plates as a guide.) Sprinkle a cookie sheet with water. Place the smaller sheet on top of the larger sheet and brush with beaten egg. Bake pastry in a 400° oven for 20 to 25 minutes until the pastry is puffed and golden, or bake a prepared pie shell and serve this dish as a one crust pie. Place the wine, water, clam broth, onion slices and lemon in a skillet. Add the fish fillets, scallops and shrimp. Bring to simmering point and poach fish for 8 minutes. Remove fish. Strain the poaching liquid into a clean saucepan and boil until 1¼ cups liquid remain. Sauté mushrooms for 5 minutes in 1 tablespoon butter and lemon juice.

To make the sauce:
Melt the butter in a small saucepan. Stir in the flour. Add the reduced poaching liquid gradually. Add parsley. Combine egg yolks and cream and add to the sauce. Remove sauce from heat and stir in mushrooms. If you are making a two crust pie, remove the top crust. Place the flounder, scallops and clams in the pastry shell. Spoon the sauce over the fish. Arrange the shrimp round the edge of the pastry. Cover with the top circle of pastry. Bake in a preheated 400° oven for 5 minutes and serve hot.

Terrine de poulet

Terrine of chicken

8 servings

   1 pound (3 cups) cooked
     chicken, turkey or game
   1 pound sausage meat
½ pound sliced boiled ham,
     diced
   2 cloves garlic, crushed
   2 eggs
   1 teaspoon tarragon
   1 tablespoon parsley, finely
     chopped
¼ cup brandy
½ teaspoon salt
     Freshly ground black pepper
½ cup butter, softened
½ pound bacon, thinly sliced

Cut chicken into small pieces
and put aside. Mix together the
sausage meat, ham, garlic, eggs,
tarragon, parsley, brandy,
salt, pepper and butter. Line a
one and a half quart casserole
with three quarters of the
bacon. Top with a layer of
sausage mixture and then a
layer of chicken. Repeat until
all the ingredients are used.
Top with a layer of sausage.
Cover with remaining bacon.
Cover the casserole. Place in a
pan of hot water and bake in
a 375° oven for two hours.
Chill for at least four hours
before slicing. Serve with
freshly made toast.

Pâté de volaille

Chicken pâté

10 servings

1¼ pounds boneless cooked
     chicken or turkey
½ pound cooked pork
½ pound cooked ham
   2 cloves garlic, crushed
   3 scallions, finely chopped
   1 medium sized onion, finely
     chopped
   1 tablespoon parsley, finely
     chopped
   1 bay leaf
¼ teaspoon thyme
½ teaspoon salt
     Freshly ground black pepper
   2 eggs, lightly beaten
   1 tablespoon flour
½ cup butter, softened
¼ cup brandy
½ pound bacon

Grind or chop the chicken,
pork and ham into very small
pieces. Add garlic and scallions,
onion, parsley, bay leaf and
thyme. Season with salt and
pepper. Add eggs, flour, butter
and brandy to the meat mixture.
Stir until well combined. Line
a 1½ quart casserole with
bacon slices. Add the meat
mixture and top with remaining
bacon. Cover casserole and
place in a pan of hot water.
Bake in a 350° oven for 1 hour.
Remove pâté from the oven.
Place a weight on top of the
pâté. Refrigerate for at least
one day before slicing.

Oeufs au crevettes

Foie de poulet

Quiche Lorraine

Eggs with shrimp

6 servings

- *6 hard boiled eggs*
- *3 tablespoons butter*
- *3 scallions, finely chopped*
- *1 tablespoon parsley, finely chopped*
- *½ teaspoon tarragon*
- *1 cup small shrimp, chopped into small pieces*
- *1 tablespoon mild (Dijon) mustard*
- *½ cup heavy cream*
  Pinch salt
  Freshly ground black pepper
- *3 tablespoons grated Parmesan cheese*
- *1 teaspoon additional butter*

Chop eggs finely. Sauté scallions in hot butter. Add eggs, parsley, tarragon, shrimp, mustard and heavy cream. Season with salt and pepper. Heat mixture for 3 minutes. Place in a buttered baking dish or individual small dishes. Sprinkle with grated cheese, dot with butter and place under a preheated grill for 3 minutes until bubbling hot and lightly browned. Serve with freshly made toast.

Chicken livers flamed in brandy

6 servings

- *2 tablespoons butter*
- *½ yellow onion, finely chopped*
- *1 carrot, finely diced*
- *1 pound chicken livers*
- *3 slices boiled ham, diced*
- *3 mushrooms, sliced thinly or 1 (3 ounce) can mushrooms, drained*
- *2 tablespoons brandy (opt.)*
- *2 tablespoons flour*
- *½ cup white wine and*
- *½ cup beef broth*
- *1 cup seedless green grapes*
- *2 tablespoons finely chopped parsley for garnish*

Heat the butter in a large skillet. Sauté the onion three minutes until transparent. Add carrot and continue cooking for 2 minutes. Add chicken livers and stir over high heat until almost tender. Add ham and mushrooms and cook two minutes. Add brandy and light it with a match immediately. When the flames have died down, stir in the flour and add wine and broth gradually, to form a medium thick sauce. Add grapes and cook just until the grapes have heated through. Garnish with parsley.

Bacon and egg pie

6 servings

Pastry:
- *1¼ cups sifted all purpose flour*
- *½ teaspoon salt*
- *3 tablespoons butter or margarine, cut into small pieces*
- *3 tablespoons cooking fat*
- *3 tablespoons ice water*

Filling:
- *½ pound bacon*
- *¼ pound (1 cup) Swiss cheese, grated*
- *4 eggs*
- *1 tablespoon flour*
- *1¼ cups milk or half and half or heavy cream*
- *½ teaspoon salt*
  Freshly ground black pepper
- *1 tablespoon butter, melted*

Measure flour and salt into a bowl. Add butter or margarine and fat. Combine with a pastry blender or fingertips. Add water a little at a time. Stir with a fork and form pastry in a ball. Wrap in wax paper and chill for 20 minutes. Roll on a lightly floured board and fit pastry into a nine inch pie plate.

Filling:
Fry bacon until crisp. Drain and crumble the bacon. Place in the uncooked pastry shell with grated cheese. In a small bowl combine eggs, flour, milk or cream, salt and pepper. Pour over the bacon and cheese. Add melted butter. Bake in a preheated 375° oven for 30 minutes until custard is firm and golden. Serve hot or cold.

In prehistoric caves discovered in France, ancient fossils of snail shells have been found alongside the fossilized remains of fish bones and oyster shells. Very good circumstantial evidence that the taste for snails must be as old as mankind itself. The ancient Romans had extensive snail farms. The Roman snail farmer Fulvius Hirpinus imported young snails from Africa and the Balkans for Roman gourmets and raised them in large earthenware pots. To enhance their flavor he fed them a steady diet of wheat flour which had been cooked in wine to make a kind of porridge. Roman cooks made a very delicious dish out of the snails with a piquant sauce of olive oil, wine, anchovies, pepper and cumin.

The best and most delicious snails of France come from the vineyards of Burgundy and Alsace. But snails are loved so much both in France and abroad that the French vineyards cannot produce enough of them and the French have to import a large number from Turkey.

After snails are caught they are left to fast for a certain period so that they can get rid of any poisonous foods they may have eaten. They are then cooked in a little ash and water while still in their shells, removed from the shells and cooked again with garlic, onion, and preferably a dash of brandy. The shells are then very carefully washed. If the snails are not used immediately, they are canned or frozen and the shells are packed separately in bags. Snails can be bought in this way in delicatessens and gourmet food stores all over the world. They need only be heated with butter and herbs. In France, however, people prefer to cook snails fresh, and in the country people still believe that there is no better cough medicine than snail broth.

Escargots à la Bourguignonne

Snails in wine

4 servings

  ⅔ *cup butter*
  3 *anchovy fillets*
  2 *scallions, finely chopped*
  2 *tablespoons parsley, finely chopped*
  2 *cloves garlic, crushed*
  1 *tablespoon brandy or Pernod (opt.)*
  1 *package (24) snails and shells*
  2 *tablespoons fine bread crumbs*
  2 *tablespoons white wine*

Beat the butter with a wooden spoon until softened. Rinse anchovies in cold water to remove excess salt. Pat anchovies dry on paper towels. Mash anchovies and add to the butter. Add scallions, parsley, garlic and brandy to butter. Chill butter one hour until firm. Place a teaspoon of butter in each shell. Slip a snail into each shell and seal in place with remaining butter. Press breadcrumbs onto the butter. Place snails in snail dishes; or crumble aluminum foil and spread on a cookie sheet.
Place shells in depressions in the foil to prevent them from tipping. Sprinkle white wine over shells. Bake in a 375° oven for 8 minutes. (If the snails are prepared in snail dishes but without shells, bake for only 5 minutes).
Serve hot.

Artichauts vinaigrette

Artichokes vinaigrette

6 servings

  6 *artichokes*
  ½ *lemon*
  1 *teaspoon salt*

Vinaigrette sauce:
  ½ *teaspoon salt*
     Freshly ground black pepper
  1 *clove garlic, crushed*
  ½ *teaspoon mild (Dijon) mustard*
  2 *tablespoons vinegar*
  6 *tablespoons light olive oil or salad oil*
  3 *tablespoons parsley, finely chopped*
  3 *tablespoons chives, finely chopped*
  1 *tablespoon capers*
  1 *tablespoon sweet gherkins, finely chopped*
  1 *hard boiled egg, finely chopped*

Cut off the artichoke stems very close to the bottom. This will enable them to stand without tipping when they are served. Remove any blemished outer leaves. Snip off the point of each leaf with a pair of scissors, cutting about ¼ inch down each leaf. Plunge artichokes into a large pot of simmering salted water. Add lemon half. Cover and simmer 45 minutes or until a leaf will pull away easily. Combine the ingredients for the vinaigrette sauce in the order listed. Serve sauce in individual small containers. Serve artichokes hot or cold.

Soups

Soupe à l'oignon

Onion soup

4 servings

- 3 tablespoons butter
- 3 large onions, thinly sliced
- 1 tablespoon flour
- ½ teaspoon salt
  Freshly ground black pepper
- 5 cups beef broth
- 4 thick slices French or
  Italian bread
- 4 tablespoons grated
  Parmesan cheese
- 4 tablespoons grated Swiss
  or Gruyère cheese

In a heavy pan, melt the butter, add the sliced onions and cook slowly stirring occasionally, until golden. Sprinkle on the flour and stir for a few minutes to cook the flour. Season with salt and pepper. Add the broth, stirring constantly. Bring to a boil, lower the heat and let the soup simmer, partially covered, for 30 minutes. Toast the slices of bread in the oven until brown. Place them in a large ovenproof soup tureen or individual bowls. Preheat the grill. Sprinkle the bread with Parmesan cheese. Pour the soup over the bread and top with the Swiss or Gruyère cheese. Brown the cheese under the grill and serve immediately.

Onion soup is, among its other virtues, considered a delicious remedy for a hangover after an evening of drinking. In Paris' better days the small bistros near the 'Halles', the splendid open-air market of the capital, had an early-morning clientele of partygoers in evening dress who mixed gaily with butchers and porters to share the benefits of onion soup. In those days the market was still held in the middle of the street and at night fresh fish, meat and vegetables arrived from the provinces. The bistros stayed open all night to serve wine and soup.

Velouté laitue

Cream of lettuce soup

6 servings

    3 heads lettuce
    2 tablespoons butter
1½ teaspoons salt
       Freshly ground black pepper
    4 cups water
½ cup heavy cream
       Juice of ½ lemon
    6 thick slices French or
       Italian bread, toasted

Wash the lettuce, remove the
cores and quarter the heads.
Cook in boiling, lightly salted
water for 10 minutes. Drain
and chop the lettuce roughly.
Melt the butter in a saucepan.
add the lettuce, cover with a
circle of wax paper and cook
slowly for 5 minutes. Remove
the paper and sprinkle lettuce
with the salt and pepper; add
the water and bring to a boil.
Lower the heat and simmer,
partially covered, for 1 hour.
Purée the soup in a blender
or force through a sieve.
Return it to the pan, add the
cream and lemon juice, and
heat thoroughly before
serving. Float a round of
toasted bread in each bowl.
You may also chill the soup
for several hours and serve
it cold.

Potage paysanne

Vegetable soup

6 servings

½ pound lean bacon, cubed
    6 small breakfast sausages
    1 onion, finely chopped
    3 medium onions, halved
    2 pounds potatoes, cubed
½ pound carrots, cubed
    1 teaspoon salt
       Freshly ground black pepper
5½ cups beef broth
½ pound fresh or frozen
       green peas
½ pound fresh or frozen
       green beans

In a large heavy pot, cook the
bacon until crisp and the
sausages until brown.
Remove the sausages and
drain on paper towels. Strain
off all the fat from the pan,
add the onions, potatoes,
carrots, salt and pepper to the
bacon and combine thoroughly.
Lower the heat, cover and
simmer for 20 minutes. Pour
in the broth; add the peas,
beans and drained sausages,
bring to a boil, cover and
simmer 20 minutes more.
Skim the fat from the soup or
refrigerate overnight and
lift off the congealed fat. Serve
the soup hot, placing a sausage
and an onion half in each
bowl. This soup is really a
meal in itself.

Garbure

Country style vegetable soup

8 servings

*4½ pounds vegetables in season
such as: courgettes, cabbage,
carrots, string beans, bell
peppers, leeks, turnips,
broccoli*
*1 piece cooked ham (about
½ pound)*
*1 piece lean bacon (about
½ pound)*
*½ teaspoon salt
Freshly ground black pepper*
1 bay leaf
½ teaspoon thyme
1 tablespoon chopped parsley
½ teaspoon dried marjoram
3 cloves garlic, crushed
*2 ounces prosciutto or
country ham, cut into small
pieces
Slices of rye bread*

Clean the vegetables and cut
into rough pieces. Place the
ham and bacon, fat side up,
in a large heavy pan. Add all
the vegetables (except cabbage,
if used), salt, pepper, bay leaf,
thyme, parsley, marjoram and
garlic; almost cover with
water and bring to a boil.
Lower the heat, cover the pan
and simmer 2 hours. Add the
proscuitto and cabbage, if used.
Cover and simmer another
hour. Strain the broth into a
warm soup tureen. Cut the
bacon and ham into pieces and
place the meats and vegetables
in a warm dish. In individual
soup bowls, place a slice of
rye bread, top with some of
the meat and vegetables and
pour over the hot broth.

Potage crécy

Carrot soup

4 servings

3 tablespoons butter
*1 pound carrots, peeled and
diced*
1 small onion, chopped
*1 medium sized potato,
peeled and diced*
*½ teaspoon salt
Freshly ground black pepper*
½ teaspoon sugar
3 cups beef broth
1 tablespoon chopped parsley
*1 teaspoon chopped chervil
or marjoram*

Melt the butter in a heavy
saucepan, add the carrots,
onion, and potato. Season with
the salt, pepper and sugar.
Cover and cook over low heat
for 15 minutes. Add the
broth and bring to a boil.
Lower the heat, cover and
simmer for another 15 minutes.
Purée the soup in a blender or
force it through a sieve. Serve
the soup hot, garnishing each
serving with some of the
chopped herbs.

Soupe au potiron

Pumpkin soup

6 servings

3 tablespoons butter
*1 medium onion, finely
chopped*
5 cups chicken broth
*1 teaspoon salt
Freshly ground black pepper*
1 (1 pound) can pumpkin
½ cup heavy cream

Melt the butter in a heavy
saucepan and cook the onion
over moderate heat until soft.
Add the broth, salt and
pepper and bring to a boil.
Add the pumpkin, combine it
thoroughly, lower the heat
and simmer, covered for 45
minutes. Add the cream and
heat through. Serve hot.

Potage Parmentier

Potato soup

6 servings

4 cups chicken broth
½ teaspoon salt
*4 medium sized all purpose
potatoes*
3 yellow onions, chopped
*3 fresh leeks, chopped or
1 additional onion*
*½ teaspoon chervil or
marjoram*
*2 tablespoons parsley,
finely chopped*
½ cup heavy cream
1 tablespoon butter

Bring chicken broth to
simmering point and add salt.
Peel potatoes and cut into
eights. Add potatoes, onions
and leeks to broth. Cover and
simmer for 20 minutes. Mash
potatoes into the broth using
a potato masher to form
small pieces of potato. Add
chervil or marjoram, parsley
and cream. Add butter and
serve hot.
Note: To make vichyssoise,
purée the soup in a blender
adding one additional teaspoon
of salt. Chill the soup for at
least 4 hours. Add ½ cup
more chicken broth if soup
appears too thick.

Potage Saint Germain

Fresh pea soup

4 servings

    1 lettuce
  ¼ pound butter
    2 pounds unshelled peas or
        1 package frozen peas
  ½ teaspoon salt
    1 teaspoon sugar
    4 cups water
        Freshly ground black pepper

Wash lettuce and shred leaves
into strips. Melt the butter
in a saucepan. Add lettuce,
shelled peas, salt and sugar.
Cover and simmer over low
heat for 10 minutes. Add
water and simmer another 10
minutes until the peas are
tender. Purée the soup in a
blender. Return to a clean
saucepan. Add pepper. Bring
soup to simmering point.
Serve hot.

Elzekaria

Soup from Alsace

6 servings

  ⅓ cup lard or rendered
        bacon fat
    1 large onion, finely chopped
    1 medium white cabbage
    2 cloves garlic, crushed
1½ teaspoons salt
        Freshly ground black pepper
  ½ pound kidney beans,
        soaked overnight and
        drained
    1 tablespoon cider vinegar

Heat the lard in a heavy pan
and cook the onions until
brown. Wash the cabbage and
chop into large pieces. When
the onions are golden, add the
cabbage and garlic and cook
slowly for a few minutes.
Sprinkle with the salt and
pepper, add the beans and
cover with water. Bring to a
boil, lower the heat, cover and
simmer for 3 hours. Just before
serving add the vinegar
and serve hot.

Potage de tomates

Fresh tomato soup

6 servings

    2 tablespoons butter
    1 yellow onion, finely chopped
    1 clove garlic, crushed
    5 red ripe tomatoes, quartered
    1 tablespoon tomato paste
    4 cups chicken broth
    1 bay leaf
    1 teaspoon basil
        Juice ½ lemon
  ½ teaspoon salt
        Freshly ground black pepper
    2 tablespoons parsley, finely
        chopped, for garnish

Sauté onion and garlic in hot
butter for three minutes until
softened. Add quartered
tomatoes, tomato paste,
chicken broth, bay leaf and
basil. Cover and simmer for
twenty minutes. Purée the
soup in a blender and strain
into a clean saucepan. Add
lemon juice, salt and pepper.
Return soup to simmering point
and garnish with chopped
parsley.

Sauces

The garlic sauce 'aioli' was originally served to accompany the fish cooked in the bouillabaisse. Today this lively garlic sauce is also used as a dip with raw vegetables, shellfish and the like.

Aioli

Garlic mayonnaise

Makes 2 cups

¼ cup breadcrumbs
3 teaspoons tarragon or
  wine vinegar
6 cloves garlic, crushed
¼ teaspoon salt
3 egg yolks
1½ cups olive oil or salad oil
3 tablespoons boiling
  bottled clam juice
3 tablespoons lemon juice

Place breadcrumbs in the blender. Add vinegar, garlic and salt. Add egg yolks. Turn on the motor and add oil in a steady continuous drizzle of drops. (Do not add the oil too quickly or the sauce will not thicken.) Add boiling clam juice and lemon juice. Serve with fish or vegetables.

Sauce vinaigrette

Sauce Béarnaise

Sauce velouté

French dressing

¼ teaspoon salt
   Freshly ground black pepper
1 *teaspoon mild (Dijon)*
   mustard
2 *scallions, finely chopped or*
1 *teaspoon onion, finely*
   chopped
1 *tablespoon parsley, finely*
   chopped
2 *tablespoons wine vinegar*
6 *tablespoons olive oil or*
   salad oil

Combine salt, pepper, mustard,
scallions, onion, parsley and
vinegar in a bowl. Add oil
and stir until well blended.
French dressing may be used
not only for tossed green
salads but also to marinate
cold cooked vegetables such
as asparagus, broccoli,
cauliflower and peas.
It is also very good with
cold meats and fish.

Béarnaise sauce

¼ *cup white wine*
¼ *cup tarragon or wine*
   vinegar
1 *teaspoon dried tarragon*
2 *tablespoons scallions,*
   finely chopped
⅔ *cup butter*
3 *egg yolks*
⅛ *teaspoon salt*
   Freshly ground black pepper
½ *teaspoon dried tarragon*

Place wine, wine vinegar,
tarragon and scallions in a
saucepan. Boil uncovered
until the liquid is reduced
to 2 tablespoons. Strain and
reserve liquid. Reserve 2
tablespoons of butter. Heat
the remaining butter until
very hot. Remove butter from
the heat. Beat egg yolks in a
small saucepan until slightly
thickened. Add strained wine
and vinegar. Place pan over
moderate heat. Add one
tablespoon cold reserved butter
and cook until butter has
melted, stirring constantly.
Add second tablespoon of
reserved butter and continue
stirring until butter has melted.
Remove the pan from the heat.
Add hot butter a little at a
time, stirring rapidly. Season
sauce with salt, pepper and
tarragon. Béarnaise sauce is
served with broiled steaks
and fish.

Velouté sauce

2 *tablespoons butter*
4 *level tablespoons flour*
1½ *cups chicken broth*
1 *egg yolk*
1 *teaspoon lemon juice*
⅛ *teaspoon salt*
   Freshly ground black pepper

Melt the butter and stir in
the flour. Cook over low heat
for one minute. Add chicken
broth gradually, stirring with
a whisk. Simmer one minute
until the sauce has thickened.
Add egg yolk, lemon juice
salt and pepper. Velouté sauce
may also be made with fish
stock, (or ¾ cup clam broth
combined with ¾ water) if
the sauce is to be served with
fish. Beef broth can be
substituted for chicken broth
for beef dishes.

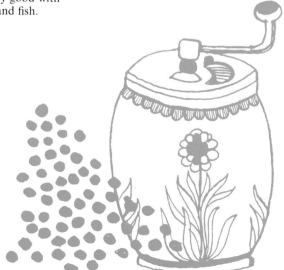

Sauce Hollandaise

Hollandaise sauce

⅔ cup butter
3 egg yolks
⅛ teaspoon salt
   Freshly ground black pepper
2 tablespoons lemon juice

Reserve 2 tablespoons butter.
Heat the remaining butter
until very hot. Remove butter
from the heat. Beat egg yolks,
salt, pepper and 1 tablespoon
lemon juice in a small saucepan
until slightly thickened. Place
pan over moderate heat.
Add one tablespoon cold
reserved butter and cook until
butter has melted, stirring
constantly. Add second
tablespoon of reserved butter
and continue stirring until
butter has melted. Remove
the pan from the heat. Add
hot butter a little at a time,
stirring rapidly. Add remaining
tablespoon of lemon juice.

Sauce ravigotte

Ravigotte sauce

1 cup oil
¼ cup red wine vinegar
¼ teaspoon salt
   Freshly ground black pepper
2 teaspoons mild (Dijon)
   mustard
1 tablespoon capers
1 shallot or scallion, finely
   chopped
2 tablespoons combined
   finely chopped fresh herbs
   (parsley, chives, tarragon,
   chervil) or 1 tablespoon
   dried herbs
1 clove garlic, crushed
1 hard-boiled egg, finely
   chopped (opt.)

In a small bowl, combine the
oil, vinegar, salt, pepper and
mustard and beat with a wire
whisk or fork until well
blended. Add the remaining
ingredients and beat until well
combined.

Sauce Béchamel

Béchamel sauce

4 tablespoons butter
4 level tablespoons flour
1½ cups milk or light cream
⅛ teaspoon salt
   Dash nutmeg

Melt the butter and stir in the
flour. Cook over low heat for
one minute. Add milk gradually
stirring constantly. Continue
cooking over moderate heat
for two minutes until the sauce
has thickened. Season with
salt and nutmeg. White sauce
is served with vegetables
(e.g. cauliflower, squash,
broccoli and endives).

Sauce Mornay

Mornay sauce

To prepare Mornay sauce, follow the directions for Béchamel sauce in the previous recipe and add ½ cup grated Swiss cheese. Mornay sauce is served with eggs, vegetables and pasta such as macaroni.

Sauce mousseline

Mousseline sauce

To prepare mousseline sauce, follow the directions for Hollandaise sauce in the previous recipe and add ½ cup heavy cream. Mousseline sauce is served with poached fish.

Sauce Espagnole

Classic brown sauce

2⅓ cups brown broth, (see page 29) or 3 beef bouillon cubes dissolved in 2⅓ cups boiling water
⅔ cup dry red wine
3 tablespoons butter
3 tablespoons flour
1 teaspoon tomato paste

Place the broth and wine in a saucepan and boil until reduced to 1½ cups. In another heavy saucepan, melt the butter and add the flour. Stir with a wire whisk and cook for 3 to 4 minutes or until the flour is light brown. Add the bouillon/wine mixture gradually, beating with a wire whisk. Return the sauce to the simmer and cook until thick. Beat in the tomato paste. Brown sauce is used to accompany braised meats, game and steaks.

Sauce Madère

Madeira sauce

Prepare Sauce Espagnole and add 2 tablespoons Madeira. Just before serving, beat in 1 tablespoon butter.

Mayonaise

Sauce verte

Mayonnaise

3 egg yolks
1/4 teaspoon dry mustard
   powder
1/2 teaspoon salt
   Freshly ground black pepper
3 tablespoons lemon juice
   or red wine vinegar or a
   combination of the two
1 1/2 cups olive oil or salad oil

Place the egg yolks in a bowl.
Using a hand or standard
electric mixer or a wire whisk,
beat the yolks until they are
thick and creamy. Beat in the
mustard powder, salt, pepper
and 1 tablespoon lemon juice
or vinegar. Add the oil in a
slow, steady, continuous
stream of drops, beating
constantly, until all the oil is
used and the mayonnaise is
thick. Be sure not to add the
oil too quickly or the
mayonnaise may curdle. Beat
in the remaining lemon juice
or vinegar. If the mixture
curdles, beat an egg yolk in
another bowl until it is thick
and creamy. Add the curdled
mayonnaise by droplets,
beating continuously. Continue
until you have beaten all the
curdled mayonnaise into the
fresh egg yolk.

Green mayonnaise

Prepare mayonnaise as
directed. Beat in 3 to 4
tablespoons finely chopped
combined green herbs such as
parsley, chives, chervil,
tarragon, basil, oregano or
boiled spinach.

Bouillon blanc de veau

Bouillon de poisson

Bouillon blanc de volaille

Bouillon brun

White beef broth

1–2 pounds veal bones with meat attached, the same herbs, vegetables and liquid used for white chicken broth. Follow the directions given for white chicken broth (page 29).

Fish broth

   1 pound fish trimmings (heads, bones, fins, etc.)
   1 slice lemon
   3 parsley stems
   1 small onion, thinly sliced
   1 small carrot, chopped
   ¼ teaspoon salt
   5 peppercorns
   4 fresh mushroom stems, chopped (optional)
   ½ cup dry white wine or dry vermouth
   3 cups cold water

Place all the ingredients in a saucepan. Bring slowly to a simmer and simmer very slowly over low heat for 45 minutes. Strain and cool.

White chicken broth

1–2 pounds chicken backs, necks, wings, hearts, gizzards
   1 large onion, washed but unskinned, and quartered
   1 carrot, roughly cut
   2 stalks celery, roughly cut
   1 tomato, quartered
   2 bay leaves
   ½ teaspoon thyme
10 peppercorns
   3 parsley stalks
   2 quarts water

Place all the ingredients in a large pot and bring to a boil. Lower the heat, partially cover the pot and let simmer very slowly for 3 hours. Strain the broth. Chill it in the refrigerator and lift off the fat before using the broth.

Brown broth

1–2 pounds beef or veal (or both) bones with meat attached
   1 large onion, washed but unskinned, and quartered
   1 carrot, roughly cut
   2 stalks celery, roughly cut
   1 tomato, quartered
   2 bay leaves
   ½ teaspoon thyme
10 peppercorns
   3 parsley stalks
   2 quarts water

Place the bones with meat in a roasting pan and brown for 15 minutes in a 400° oven. Add the vegetables and continue browning for 10 minutes. Transfer the bones, meat and vegetables to a large pot, add the herbs and water and bring to a boil. Reduce the heat, partially cover the pot and simmer very slowly for 4 to 5 hours. Only an occasional bubble should break the surface. Strain the broth, chill it in the refrigerator and lift off the fat before using the broth.

Fish dishes

The great French connoisseur, writer and epicure of the table, Brillat Savarin, wrote that 'fish is the most inexhaustible source of culinary inspiration there is'. French cooks have always known how to use this source of inspiration very well. It is extraordinary what the French can do with the simplest and cheapest fish. To begin with, the French demand fish that is very fresh and go out of their way to obtain it. Very early in the morning at one of Paris' main stations you can see cooks from the small fish restaurants arrive to meet the trains coming from Brittany. There they personally take charge of the baskets of fresh fish from the Breton ports so that they can get it to their kitchens immediately.

King Louis XV is supposed to have awarded a prize of 9,000 gold francs for an absolutely fresh gilthead, and the absence of fresh fish was once the direct cause of a dramatic suicide: In 1671 the Prince of Condé planned a feast for King Louis XIV and some 3,000 other distinguished guests. When the fresh fish failed to arrive in time, the butler, Vatel, felt himself so disgraced that he stabbed himself with his sword.

Appropriately enough, the most famous fish restaurant in the world is Prunier in Paris. In the basement kitchen, chef Charles Verdilhac stands like a magician behind an enormous stove in which a coal fire roars and glows (the great French cooks still cook on coal stoves and will have nothing to do with electricity and gas!). Although one might imagine that the formidable chef saves his best efforts for expensive fish such as lobster, sole and turbot, the master runs a democratic kitchen and prepares simple whiting, cod and mussels with the same care that he reserves for the more aristocratic species of the water kingdom. According to tradition, Parisian connoisseurs dine at Prunier twice a year: once early in autumn, when the chestnut trees along the wide boulevards turn yellow, to taste the oysters, and once in April, when the first young leaves of the same chestnut trees appear, to eat fresh caviar from the Gironde accompanied by a fine, soft sparkling champagne to celebrate the beginning of spring.

Cotriade

Fish soup

6 servings

- 3 pounds fish: such as a combination of sea bass, mullet, haddock, mackerel, devil fish, whiting, sardine
- 2 tablespoons olive oil
- 2 large onions, chopped
- 6 cups fish broth (see page 29) or 3 chicken bouillon cubes dissolved in 6 cups water
- 2 teaspoons salt
  Freshly ground black pepper
- 1 tablespoon parsley, finely chopped
- 1/4 teaspoon dried sage
- 1/4 teaspoon marjoram
- 1/4 teaspoon dried thyme
- 1 bay leaf
- 1 pound potatoes cut into large cubes
  French or Italian bread

Clean the fish and cut into thick slices. In a large pan, heat the oil, add the onions and sauté over medium heat until brown. Add the broth and bring to a boil over high heat. Add the salt, pepper, parsley, sage, marjoram, thyme and bay leaf and simmer 3 minutes. Add the potatoes, cover and cook over medium heat 5 to 7 minutes. Add the fish slices, lower the heat and cook, covered, for 7 to 10 minutes or until the fish flakes easily. Place fish on a warm platter and surround with the potatoes. Place thick slices of bread in individual soup bowls and pour over the bouillon.

Bar poché

Poached bass

6 servings

- 1 (4 pound) whole bass, cleaned
- 3 tablespoons lemon juice
- 1/2 teaspoon salt
  Freshly ground black pepper
- 1/2 teaspoon either chervil, tarragon or dill
- 2 tablespoons butter, melted
- 2 cups milk
- 1/2 onion, sliced
- 1/2 carrot, chopped
- 1 stalk celery, chopped
- 1 bay leaf
- 1/2 teaspoon peppercorns
- 2 tablespoons butter
- 2 tablespoons flour
- 2 tablespoons parsley, finely chopped

Season fish inside and on the surface with lemon juice, salt, pepper and chervil. Add half of the butter inside the fish and brush skin with the remaining butter. Place fish in a baking dish. Pour in the milk and add onion, carrot, celery, bay leaf and peppercorns. Cover with foil and bake 25 minutes in a 350° oven. Remove the fish and keep it warm. Strain milk. Melt remaining 2 tablespoons butter in a saucepan. Stir in the flour and add the milk gradually. Spoon the sauce over the fish and garnish with parsley.

Saumon poché

Poached salmon

4 servings

   1 *cup dry white wine*
   2 *cups water*
   1 *medium onion, sliced*
   2 *carrots, sliced*
¾ *teaspoon salt*
   1 *bay leaf*
   4 *salmon steaks*
      Watercress
      Hollandaise sauce (page 26)

Place the wine, water, onion, carrots, salt and bay leaf in a heavy saucepan. Bring to a boil, lower the heat and simmer 45 minutes. Place the salmon in a lightly buttered shallow pan, strain on the liquid and cover with buttered wax paper cut to fit the pan. Bring the liquid to a simmer on top of the stove, place in a 375° oven and poach for 10–15 minutes depending on the thickness of the steaks. Drain the fish and place on a serving platter. Garnish with watercress and serve warm with Hollandaise sauce.

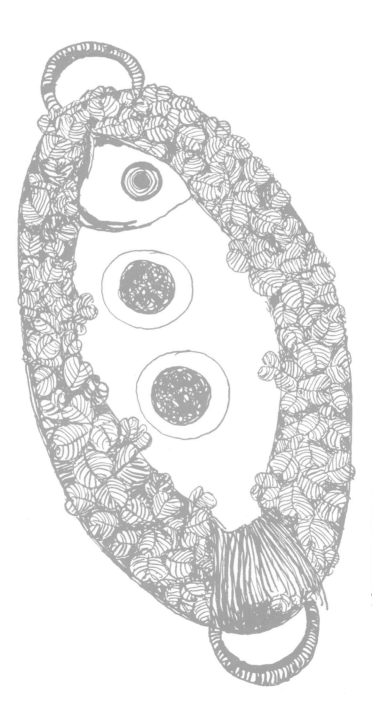

Salade de tourteau

Crab salad

6 servings

   2 *pounds crabmeat, cleaned*
   6 *mushrooms, sliced*
   2 *tablespoons lemon juice*
   6 *tablespoons olive oil or vegetable oil*
¼ *teaspoon salt*
      Freshly ground black pepper
   4 *hard boiled eggs*
   2 *tomatoes, cut into wedges*
   2 *green peppers, cut into strips*
 12 *black olives, pitted*
¼ *cup English walnuts, chopped*
   2 *tablespoons parsley, finely chopped*

Combine crabmeat and mushrooms in a bowl. Stir together the lemon juice, oil, salt and pepper. Moisten crabmeat and mushrooms with 2 tablespoons lemon juice and oil. Place crabmeat in the center of a serving dish. Cut eggs into wedges and arrange around the crabmeat. Place tomatoes in a bowl. Simmer green pepper strips for four minutes in boiling water. Drain and rinse in cold water. Add green pepper and olives to tomatoes. Toss with remaining lemon juice and oil. Drain and arrange around crabmeat. Sprinkle crabmeat with walnuts and parsley.

Sole à la Normande

Sole Normandy style

4 servings

16 mussels, fresh or canned
½ pound mushrooms, washed,
    trimmed and quartered
    if large
4 tablespoons water
    Juice of one lemon
3 tablespoons butter
1 teaspoon salt
½ pound shrimp, cooked,
    shelled and deveined
2 packages frozen puff
    pastry, thawed
2 cups fish broth, shrimp
    cooking liquid or 2 chicken
    bouillon cubes, dissolved
    in 2 cups water
4 fillets of sole, about 1½
    pounds, folded in half
2½ tablespoons flour
2 egg yolks
⅓ cup heavy cream
    Sprigs of parsley
1 black truffle, thinly
    sliced (optional)

If using fresh mussels, clean
as described in the recipe for
moules marinière (page 42).
Steam in ½ cup water until
the shells open. Discard shells
and wrap mussels in aluminum
foil. In a saucepan, combine
the mushrooms, water, lemon
juice, 1 tablespoon butter
and salt. Cover with a circle
of wax paper and cook over
low heat for about 7 minutes.
Drain and reserve the liquid.
Wrap mushrooms in aluminum
foil. Wrap the shrimp in foil.
Roll out the thawed pastry
to make 1 sheet of dough
about ⅛″ thick. Cut 12 small
crescent shapes and bake
according to package directions.
Combine the mushroom
cooking liquid with the
bouillon in a shallow pan.
Add the fillets, cover with a
piece of buttered wax paper
cut to fit the pan and bring to
a simmer on top of the stove.
Transfer to a 400° oven and
cook 5 minutes. Do not
over-cook. Carefully, transfer
the fillets to a warmed serving
dish. Turn the oven off and
place the mussels, mushrooms
and shrimp in their foil
packages and the baked
crescent pastries, uncovered,
in the oven to reheat. Over
high heat, reduce the fish
cooking liquid to 1 cup. In a
small, heavy saucepan, melt
the remaining 2 tablespoons
butter. Add the flour and
cook 1 or 2 minutes. Beat in
the reduced cooking liquid,
stirring constantly, and bring
to a simmer. Beat the egg
yolks into the cream and
add to the sauce. Do not allow
it to boil but just heat through.
Season with drops of lemon
juice and salt and pepper if
needed. Pour the sauce over
the fillets and garnish the dish
with the mussels, mushrooms,
shrimp, crescent shaped
pastries and parsley. Place
sliced truffles on the fillets.
Serve hot.

Quenelles de brochet Nantua

Fish balls in Nantua sauce

8 servings

1 pound package frozen
    fish fillets, skinned and
    boned
½ cup butter, creamed
1 teaspoon salt
    Dash of white pepper
1 cup water
¼ cup butter, cut in pieces
1 teaspoon salt
1 cup flour
3 eggs
¼ cup butter, creamed
¼ cup cooked rock lobster,
    finely chopped
2 cups Béchamel sauce,
    (page 26)

Dry the fillets very
thoroughly on paper towels.
Put them through the finest
blade of a meat grinder and
beat into the creamed butter
along with the salt and white
pepper until very well
combined. In a heavy saucepan,
bring the water, butter and
salt to a boil. (Do not allow
the water to boil before the
butter melts). Add the flour
all at once and beat over
medium heat with a spatula
until the mixture forms a
ball and leaves a slight film
on the bottom of the pan.
Cool the paste, then add it to
the perch mixture, beating
vigorously. Add the eggs,
one at a time, combining each
thoroughly before adding
another. Cover the mixture
and chill for several hours.
In a large pan, bring about
3 inches of water barely to
simmer. Roll the fish paste
into small ovals and drop
them into the water. Poach
for 15 to 20 minutes making
sure the water is barely
simmering. Remove the
quenelles with a slotted spoon
and drain on paper towels.
While the quenelles are
poaching, beat the lobster into
the ¼ cup of creamed butter.
Heat the Béchamel sauce
and beat in the lobster butter.
Cook for 2 or 3 minutes and
taste for seasoning. Place the
quenelles in a serving dish and
cover with the lobster sauce.

SMELT

HADDOCK

SOLE

TROUT

RED MULLET

RED SNAPPER

SALMON

WHITING

CARP

SEA BASS

PIKE

MUSSEL

BASS

CRAWFISH

MACKEREL

SHRIMP

CRAB

AMERICAN LOBSTER

Sole Bercy

Sole Deauvilloise

Poissons aux câpres

Fillet of sole Bercy

4 servings

1¾ pounds sole or flounder
    fillets with skin removed
½ teaspoon salt
    Freshly ground black pepper
3 scallions, finely chopped
2 tablespoons parsley,
    finely chopped
½ cup white wine
2 tablespoons butter

Season fish with salt and
pepper. Butter a large oval
baking dish. Add the scallions
and parsley. Add wine and
place the dish in a 350° oven
for 5 minutes. Take the dish
out of the oven. Arrange
fillets in a single layer in the
dish, top with pats of butter.
Cover the fish with aluminum
foil. Place in the oven for 15
minutes. Remove paper.
Drain off the poaching liquid.
Place under the grill for
2 minutes. Serve hot.

Fillet of sole au gratin in cider sauce

4 servings

¼ cup butter
½ pound onions, chopped
½ cup heavy cream
1½–2 pounds fillets of sole or
    one large flounder, head
    and tail intact
1¼ cups fish broth or 1
    chicken bouillon cube
    dissolved in 1¼ cups water
¾ cup apple cider or juice
½ teaspoon salt
    Freshly ground black pepper
    Peel of one lemon
1½ tablespoons butter
2 tablespoons flour
    Dash of nutmeg
1 teaspoon dry mustard
    Drops of lemon juice
3–4 tablespoons fine dry
    breadcrumbs

In a small saucepan, heat the
butter, add the onions and
cook until soft. Purée the
mixture in the blender with
2 tablespoons of cream or
force through a sieve. Place
the fillets, folded in half, or the
whole fish in a shallow, lightly
buttered flameproof serving
dish. Combine the broth,
cider, salt, pepper and lemon
peel and bring to a simmer.
Simmer 10 minutes and strain
onto the fish. Cover the fish
with a buttered piece of wax
paper cut to fit the pan.
Bring the liquid to a simmer on
top of the stove, place in a
400° oven and poach for 5 to
10 minutes. The whole fish
will require the longer time.

Strain off the poaching liquid
and reserve. Melt 1 tablespoon
butter, add the flour and cook
for a few minutes over medium
heat. Add 1¼ cups of the
poaching liquid, stirring
constantly until smooth. Add
the puréed onions, remaining
cream, nutmeg, mustard and
a few drops of lemon juice.
Bring to a boil, stirring,
and simmer a few minutes.
Pour the sauce over the fish,
sprinkle with breadcrumbs,
dot with butter and place
under the grill for about
2 minutes or until golden.
Garnish with parsley and
serve hot.

Fish fillets with capers

4 servings

2 pounds salt water fish
    fillets: e.g. haddock,
    cod, etc.
2 cups fish broth or 2 chicken
    bouillon cubes dissolved
    in 2 cups water
½ cup butter
    Juice of 1 lemon
½ cup capers
2 teaspoons red wine vinegar
1 tablespoon chopped parsley

Place the fillets in a lightly
buttered flameproof dish, pour
on the broth and cover with
buttered wax paper, cut to
fit the pan. Bring to a simmer
on top of the stove. Place in
a 375° oven and poach for
10–12 minutes or until the fish
flakes easily. While the fish
cooks, melt the butter in a
small pan, stir in the lemon
juice, capers, and vinegar and
heat until bubbling. When the
fish is done, drain it and
place on a warmed serving
dish. Pour the butter over and
garnish with chopped parsley.

Homard à l'Armoricaine

Crevettes à la crème

In France, anything that has to do with good eating and drinking is taken so seriously that gourmets and gastronomical writers can deliberate endlessly over the origin, composition and proper name of a particular dish. One recipe still debated by the epicures is 'Lobster à l'Armoricaine'.

This delicious dish of warm lobster in a piquant sauce of brandy, shallot, garlic, and herbs belongs to the top of the list of every great French cook – and almost every one of them has thought up his own small variation. As a result, 'Lobster à l'Armoricaine' is never eaten in quite the same way in any two restaurants.

The general concensus, at any rate, is that the dish was discovered in 1853 by a Parisian restaurant owner and that it is based on the traditional way of preparing shellfish in the south of France. No one knows the precise name that was given to the recipe at the time, though some say that it was 'Lobster à l'Américaine' in honor of some American guests at the restaurant. The more accepted view, however, is that the name 'Lobster à l'Armoricaine' originates from the word 'Armorica', the old Celtic name for Brittany, a region that still produces delicious lobster. The variant name 'Américaine', it would then appear, came much later when American tourists in Paris became so fond of this delicious dish.

Breton style lobster

6 servings

    3 (1½ pound) live lobsters
        or frozen lobster tails
    3 tablespoons butter,
        softened
    1 tablespoon olive oil
    1 tablespoon butter
    1 small onion, finely chopped
    2 scallions, finely chopped
    1 clove garlic, crushed
    3 tablespoons brandy, warmed
 1½ tablespoons flour
    2 medium sized tomatoes,
        peeled, seeded and chopped
    1 tablespoon tomato paste
    2 tablespoons parsley,
        finely chopped
    1 teaspoon tarragon
  ¼ cup bottled clam juice
  ¼ cup water
  ½ cup white wine
  ¼ teaspoon salt
        Freshly ground black pepper

Pierce live lobsters with a sharp knife at the point where the body meets the tail. Remove uncooked lobster meat. Reserve red coral and green tomalley and combine with softened butter. Keep this mixture to one side. Cut lobster, or partially thawed lobster tails, into bite-sized pieces. Heat oil and 1 tablespoon butter in a heavy skillet. Sauté onion, scallions and garlic for two minutes. Add lobster and cook over moderately high heat for 3 minutes. Add warmed brandy and light with a match. When the flames die down fold in the flour. Add tomatoes, tomato paste, parsley and

tarragon. Stir in clam juice, water and wine. Season with salt and pepper. Cover skillet and simmer for 15 minutes. Stir in reserved coral butter mixture. Simmer 2 more minutes until the sauce has thickened. Serve hot.

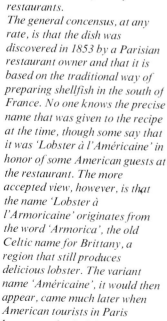

Shrimps in cream

4 servings

    4 tablespoons butter
 1½ pounds small shrimp,
        cleaned, shelled and
        deveined
  ¼ teaspoon salt
        Freshly ground black pepper
    1 tablespoon paprika
  ⅓ cup sherry or Madeira
        wine
  ¼ cup white wine
    1 cup heavy cream

Heat the butter in a skillet. Add shrimp. Season with salt, pepper and paprika and sauté over high heat for 5 minutes. Remove shrimp to a hot platter and keep warm. Add sherry or Madeira and white wine to the skillet. Boil over high heat until only about 4 tablespoons liquid remain. Add cream and continue cooking over high heat until the cream has thickened into a sauce. Pour sauce over the shrimp and serve hot. This dish is also excellent made with 2 (12 ounce) packages frozen langoustes or 1½ pounds freshly boiled lobster meat.

Merlan au vin rouge

Grenouilles

Buissons d'éperlans

Barbue Mornay

Whiting in wine sauce

4 servings

2 tablespoons olive oil
1 medium onion, finely
  chopped
1 tablespoon flour
1 cup dry red wine
1 cup water
¾ teaspoon salt
  Freshly ground black pepper
2 cloves garlic, crushed
¼ teaspoon thyme
1 bay leaf
1 tablespoon chopped parsley
2 teaspoons tomato paste
2 large whiting, cut into 1"
  thick slices
1 cup flour seasoned with
  ½ teaspoon salt
  Freshly ground black pepper
3 tablespoons olive oil
1 tablespoon capers

Heat the olive oil in a heavy
saucepan and sauté the onion
until golden. Add the flour,
stir and cook for 1 minute.
Pour on the wine and water,
stirring vigorously. Bring to a
boil and add salt, pepper,
garlic, thyme, bay leaf, parsley
and tomato paste. Lower the
heat and simmer until the
sauce is reduced to about 1¼
cups. While the sauce is
reducing, dredge the fish slices
in seasoned flour. Heat the
olive oil until it sizzles and
sauté the fish on both sides
until done and golden. Drain
on paper towels and place on
a warmed serving platter.
When the sauce is ready,
remove the bay leaf, stir in the
capers and pour over the fish.

Frog legs

4 servings

24 frog legs
½ cup milk
½ cup flour, seasoned with
  ½ teaspoon salt
  Freshly ground black pepper
3 tablespoons butter
3 cloves garlic, crushed
2 tablespoons white vermouth
2 hard boiled eggs, chopped
2 tablespoons parsley, finely
  chopped
1 teaspoon capers (optional)
2 tablespoons lemon juice

Dip frog legs in milk and then
in seasoned flour. Shake off
excess flour. Sauté frog legs
and garlic in butter for ten
minutes until lightly browned.
Transfer frog legs to a hot
serving dish. Add vermouth
to the skillet and stir in eggs,
parsley, capers and lemon
juice. Pour all these hot
ingredients over the frog legs.
Serve hot.

Fried smelts

4 servings

1½ pounds smelts or fresh
  sardines
1 cup milk
1 cup flour
  Oil for deep frying
  Salt
  Sprigs of parsley
2 lemons, thinly sliced

Clean the smelts and dry
thoroughly on paper towels.
Heat the oil to 375° or until
almost smoking. Dip the
smelts into the milk, then
the flour and fry a few at a
time, until golden brown.
As they are done, remove and
drain on paper towels. Sprinkle
with salt and keep warm.
When all are done, transfer to
a heated bowl, mounding
them slightly. Fry sprigs of
parsley, drain and garnish the
smelts with the parsley and
lemon slices.

Halibut with Mornay sauce

6 servings

3 pounds halibut steaks
2 cups water
½ teaspoon salt
2 tablespoons lemon juice
2 tablespoons butter
2 tablespoons flour
2 cups milk
¼ cup Swiss cheese, grated
¼ cup Parmesan cheese,
  grated
¼ teaspoon salt
  Freshly ground black pepper
1 teaspoon mild (Dijon)
  mustard
½ cup breadcrumbs

Place fish in a large skillet
and cover with water. Add
salt and lemon juice. Simmer
uncovered for 15 minutes until
fish is white and flakes easily.
Drain fish and keep it warm.
Melt the butter in a saucepan.
Stir in the flour and add the
milk gradually. Add cheeses
and season the sauce with salt,
pepper and mustard. Place
fish in a baking dish. Cover
with sauce and top with
breadcrumbs. Bake 5 minutes
in a 400° oven until sauce is
lightly browned and bubbling.

*Poissons aux câpres, recipe
page 34, 4th column*

*Rougets farcis aux échalotes,
recipe page 43, 1st column*

*Maquereaux au fenouil, recipe
page 42, 3rd column*

Buissons d'éperlans

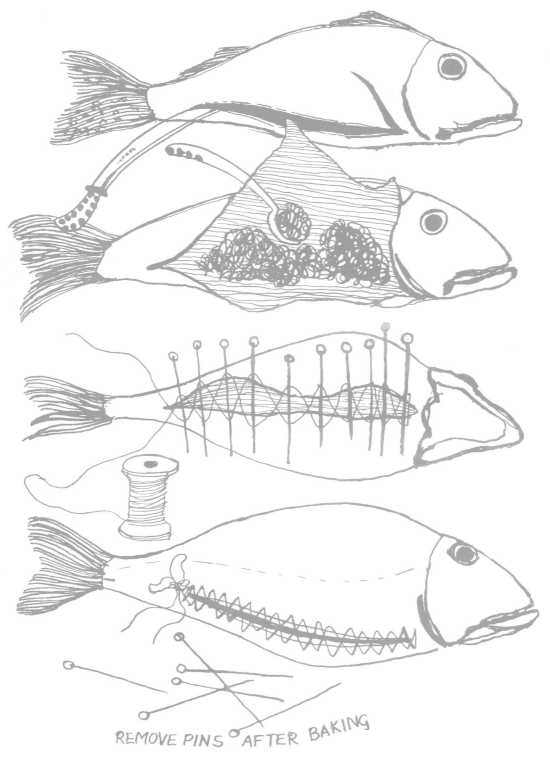

REMOVE PINS AFTER BAKING

Truite farcie

Stuffed trout

4 servings

> 4   (1 pound) trout
> ¾   cups fresh breadcrumbs
> ½   pound mushrooms, finely
>   chopped
> 1   tablespoon finely chopped
>   parsley
> 4   shallots or scallions,
>   finely chopped
> 1   teaspoon salt
>   Freshly ground black pepper
> ½   cup butter
> ¾   cup heavy cream
> ¾   cup dry white wine
> 2   medium tomatoes, peeled,
>   seeded and chopped
> ½   teaspoon salt
> ¼   teaspoon thyme
> ¼   teaspoon basil

Clean the trout, leaving the heads intact. Combine the breadcrumbs, mushrooms, parsley, 2 shallots, salt and pepper. In a heavy pan, melt 2 tablespoons of the butter and sauté the mixture until it is fairly dry. Add ¼ cup of the cream and cook a few minutes more. Dry the trout well with paper towels and stuff them with the breadcrumb mixture. Melt the remaining butter in an ovenproof serving dish, add the trout, baste with the butter and scatter the remaining chopped shallots over the fish. Cover the pan tightly with aluminum foil and bake in a 325° oven for 15 minutes. While the trout are baking, combine the remaining cream and wine in a small pan.

Saumon diable

Bouillabaisse

Bring to the simmer, add the tomatoes, salt, thyme and basil and cook for a few minutes. Remove the foil from the fish and pour on the cream mixture. Bake uncovered another 8–10 minutes. Serve hot.

Deviled salmon

4 servings

1½ *pounds salmon steaks*
½ *cup butter, softened*
1 *tablespoon mild (Dijon) mustard*
1 *tablespoon lemon juice*
  Dash cayenne pepper
2 *tablespoons parsley, finely chopped*
1½ *tablespoons vegetable oil*
¼ *teaspoon salt*
  Freshly ground black pepper

Beat butter with mustard, lemon juice, cayenne pepper and parsley. Place in the refrigerator to harden. Brush salmon with oil and season with salt and pepper. Broil 4 minutes on each side. Top hot salmon with a pat of cold flavored butter. Serve hot.

Fish soup from Marseilles

6 servings

3 *pounds assorted salt water fish (cod, haddock, sea bass, etc.)*
2 *cups bottled clam broth*
2 *cups water*
1 *onion, chopped*
2 *carrots, chopped*
2 *stalks celery, chopped*
2 *stalks parsley*
3 *tablespoons olive oil or vegetable oil*
1 *onion, finely chopped*
2 *cloves garlic, crushed*
3 *medium sized tomatoes, peeled, seeded and chopped or 1 (1 pound) can tomatoes, drained and chopped*
1 *bay leaf*
1 *teaspoon fennel seeds, crushed*
⅛ *teaspoon saffron, soaked in 1 tablespoon hot water for 5 minutes*
  Peel from ½ orange, finely chopped
½ *teaspoon salt*
  Freshly ground black pepper

Remove skin and bones from the fish. Cut fish into 2 inch slices and lay to one side. Put clam broth, water, 1 onion, carrots, celery and parsley in a large saucepan. Cover and simmer for 30 minutes. Strain the broth and discard the vegetables. Fry fish in hot oil, three minutes on each side, until lightly browned. Transfer fish to the broth. In the same skillet sauté onion and garlic for two

minutes until softened. Add tomatoes, bay leaf, fennel, saffron with its soaking water, and orange peel. Season with salt and pepper. Simmer these ingredients uncovered for 5 minutes. Transfer to the broth with the fish. Bring broth to simmering point. Ladle into soup bowls and serve with French bread.

*Cotriade, recipe page 30,
3rd column*

Truites aux amandes

Trout with almonds

4 servings

  4 (¾ *pound*) *whole trout,
     cleaned*
  1 *cup milk*
  ½ *cup flour seasoned with
     ½ teaspoon salt
     Freshly ground black pepper*
  ½ *pound butter*
  ⅓ *cup sliced almonds
     Parsley for garnish*
  1 *lemon, cut into wedges*

Dry trout with paper towels.
Dip in milk and then in flour.
Heat ¾ of the butter in a
large skillet. Fry trout four
minutes on each side over
moderate heat until golden
brown. Sprinkle fish with salt
and pepper and keep hot.
In a small skillet, heat
remaining butter and brown
the almonds. Place trout on a
hot platter. Pour the butter
and almonds over the trout.
Garnish with parsley and
lemon wedges.

Truites aux amandes

Moules marinière, recipe
page 42, 1st column

Sole à la Normande, recipe
page 32, 1st column

Seafood

There is an old French saying that fish without wine is poison, and another that says 'Fish must swim three times, once in water, then in butter, and finally in wine'. All of which confirms the classical gastronomic rule that fish and wine are inseparable. A corollary of the same rule is that fish is normally accompanied by a dry white wine. The only exception to the rule is fish prepared in a very rich sauce, with which a demi-sec white wine is drunk. A refinement of the rule is that the more delicate the fish the better the wine has to be. A fine white wine is always drunk cool – but never chilled. In fact, anything ice cold that passes over the tongue deadens the taste buds to the subtleties of the meal. A good white wine should therefore never be cooler than cellar

Moules marinière

Crevettes à l'estragon

Maquereaux au fenouil

Mussels mariners' style

6–8 servings

6–8 *dozen mussels, fresh or canned with shells, if available*
  2 *tablespoons butter*
  1 *stalk celery, chopped*
  1 *medium leek or three scallions, sliced thinly*
  1 *carrot, chopped*
  ¼ *cup chopped parsley*
  1 *bay leaf*
   Coarsley ground black pepper
  1½ *cups dry white wine*

If using fresh mussels, scrub the shells with a stiff brush, cleaning them well. Remove the beards with a sharp knife, rinse under cold running water, and soak in cold water for 10 to 15 minutes to remove excess sand. Discard any mussels that are open. In a large pot, melt the butter and cook the celery, leek or scallions, and carrot until soft. Add the remaining ingredients and bring to a simmer.
Rinse the mussels and add to the pot. Cover and steam the mussels, shaking the pan occasionally, until the shells open—about 5 to 10 minutes. Cook for 5 minutes if using canned mussels. Remove the mussels to a large warm bowl. Continue simmering the liquid for three minutes more and strain into the bowl over the mussels. Serve hot with French bread.

Shrimp with tarragon

4 servings

  2 *tablespoons butter*
  4 *scallions, finely chopped*
  2 *cloves garlic, crushed*
  2 *green peppers, finely chopped*
  1½ *pounds shrimp, shelled and deveined*
  2 *medium sized tomatoes, peeled, seeded and chopped*
  ½ *teaspoon tarragon*
  2 *tablespoons lemon juice*
  ¼ *teaspoon salt*
   Freshly ground black pepper
  ⅓ *cup white vermouth*
  ½ *cup white wine*
  1 *tablespoon cornflour, dissolved in 2 tablespoons cold water*
  2 *tablespoons parsley, finely chopped*

Cut the shrimp through the back but keep the tail attached. Heat the butter in a skillet. Sauté scallions, garlic and green pepper 3 minutes until softened. Add shrimp and cook over high heat for 3 minutes. Add tomatoes, tarragon, lemon juice, salt and pepper, vermouth and wine. Simmer 5 minutes. Stir in cornflour dissolved in cold water. Garnish with parsley and serve hot on a bed of rice.

Mackerel with fennel

6 servings

  3 *(1½ pound) mackerel*
  ¾ *cup butter, softened*
  6 *scallions, finely chopped*
  2 *tablespoons lemon juice*
  2 *tablespoons fresh fennel, or dill weed or*
  1 *teaspoon fennel seeds or dill seeds*
  1½ *tablespoons olive oil or vegetable oil*
  1 *teaspoon salt*
   Freshly ground black pepper
  6 *cherry tomatoes*

Sauce:
  ¼ *cup dry white wine*
  4 *scallions, finely chopped*
  2 *egg yolks*
  ½ *cup hot butter*
   Fennel, dill or parsley for garnish

Dry fish inside and out with paper towels. Combine butter, scallions, lemon juice and fennel. Stuff the fish with this mixture. Sew or skewer the edges together. Brush the fish with oil and sprinkle with salt and pepper. Place under the grill for ten minutes on each side. Continue cooking for ten minutes in a 400° oven. During the last five minutes add the whole tomatoes. In the meantime, prepare the sauce. Pour the wine into a small saucepan. Add the scallions and simmer over low heat for three minutes until scallions are softened and almost all the wine has boiled away. Remove the pan from the heat. Beat the egg yolks into the wine. Place the pan over very low heat. Beat in the hot butter stirring constantly. Remove the pan from the heat as soon as the sauce is thickened. Season the sauce with salt and pepper. Remove skewers from the fish and place on a hot platter. Garnish platter with tomatoes, fresh fennel, dill or parsley. Serve hot. Serve the sauce separately.

temperature (about 50°–54°). Only sweet or simple, cheap white wines are served chilled, and even then not to the point of being ice cold.

Rougets farcis aux échalotes

Stuffed striped mullet

3 servings

  3 *(one pound) striped mullets or other small salt water fish, cleaned*
¼ *pound bacon, fried until crisp, and drained*
  6 *scallions, finely chopped*
  3 *teaspoons butter, melted*
¼ *teaspoon salt*
    Freshly ground black pepper

Sauce:
  2 *tablespoons butter*
  2 *tablespoons flour*
  2 *cups milk*
  1 *tablespoon tomato paste*
¼ *cup heavy cream*
  1 *bunch parsley, finely chopped*
  9 *boiled small potatoes*

Crumble the bacon, combine with the scallions and stuff the mullets. Butter three pieces of aluminum foil and place mullets on the foil. Sprinkle with salt and pepper and fold foil into little packets. Bake in a 350° oven for 20 minutes. In the meantime, heat 2 tablespoons butter in a small saucepan. Stir in the flour and add the milk gradually. Stir in the tomato paste and cream. Season with salt and pepper. Simmer sauce, uncovered over low heat for ten minutes and then keep it warm. Take fish out of the packets and broil for 3 minutes on each side. Sprinkle parsley over a platter. Place mullets on top of the parsley and arrange the hot boiled potatoes on the platter. Serve the sauce separately.

Rougets aux fines herbes

Riviera mullet

4 servings

  2 *pounds mullet*
¼ *cup butter*
    Sprigs of parsley
  3 *shallots or scallions, finely chopped*
¼ *teaspoon dried thyme*
  1 *bay leaf*
¼ *teaspoon fennel seed*
  1 *carrot, grated*
  1 *lemon, thinly sliced*
  8 *black olives, chopped*
¼ *teaspoon salt*
    Freshly ground black pepper
  2 *teaspoons lemon juice*
½ *cup dry sherry*
  2 *tablespoons fine dry bread crumbs*
  1 *tablespoon butter*
  2 *tablespoons finely chopped parsley*

Clean the fish and dry thoroughly with paper towels. Melt the butter in an ovenproof dish large enough to hold the fish and add the parsley, shallots, thyme, bay leaf, fennel, carrot, lemon slices and olives. Season the fish inside and out with salt and pepper. Place in the dish, sprinkle with lemon juice and pour the sherry over all. Cover tightly with aluminum foil and bake in a 375° oven for 25 minutes or until done. Sprinkle the fish with bread crumbs, dot with butter and place under the broiler until the bread crumbs are golden. Sprinkle with parsley and serve hot.

Maquereaux marinés au vin blanc

Mackerel mariners' style

6 servings

>   3 pounds mackerel or
>   6 (¾ pound) trout
>   2 cups bottled clam juice
>   2 cups water
>   1 medium sized onion,
>   finely chopped
>   3 carrots, diced
>   1 teaspoon olive oil or salad oil
>   1 onion, cut into rings
>   2 carrots, thinly sliced
>   ¼ teaspoon salt
>   Freshly ground black pepper
>   1 lemon, sliced
>   1 cup dry white wine
>   1 tablespoon vinegar
>   3 tablespoons olive oil or
>   salad oil
>   ¼ teaspoon thyme
>   1 bay leaf
>   3 sprigs parsley
>   2 cloves

Pour clam juice and water into a saucepan. Add onion and carrots. Cover and simmer for 30 minutes and strain. Oil a baking dish or fish poacher. Cover the bottom with half of the onion rings and thinly sliced carrots. Place the mackerel in the dish, season with salt and pepper and cover with remaining onion and carrot. Add lemon slices. Pour in the wine, vinegar, olive oil and strained fish broth. Add the thyme, bay leaf, parsley and cloves. Cover and poach the fish over low heat for 8–10 minutes. Remove bay leaf and parsley sprigs. Allow the fish to cool completely before serving.

Estouffade de boeuf

Beef casserole

8 servings

½ pound lean sliced bacon
3½ pounds stewing steak cubed
½ cup all purpose flour
  seasoned with ¼ teaspoon
  salt
  Freshly ground pepper
2 shallots or green onions,
  sliced
2 medium sized onions,
  roughly cut
2 large carrots, thickly sliced
2 cups dry red wine
¼ cup brandy
2 cloves garlic, crushed
½ teaspoon thyme
1 bay leaf, crumbled
1 tablespoon finely chopped
  parsley
½ teaspoon salt
  Freshly ground pepper
1 tablespoon tomato paste
½–1 cup beef broth

Simmer the bacon in water
for 10 minutes to render the
fat. Drain, reserve 3 slices and
roughly chop the remainder.
In a heavy flameproof casserole
just large enough to hold the
ingredients, lay the 3 bacon
strips on the bottom. Roll the
beef cubes in seasoned flour
and place half of them close
together in a layer on top of
the bacon. Cover the beef
with half of the vegetables and
chopped bacon. Repeat the
layers with the remaining
beef, vegetables and bacon.
Warm the wine in a small pan.
Add the brandy, garlic, thyme,
bay leaf, parsley, salt, pepper
and tomato paste. Combine

thoroughly and pour into the
casserole. Use beef broth as
needed to almost cover the
contents of the pan. Bring to a
simmer on top of the stove.
Cover with aluminum foil and
then a lid and place in a 300°
oven for 3 hours. Skim off the
fat, taste for seasoning and
serve from the casserole.

Pot au feu

Beef stew

6–8 servings

    3 *pound piece of beef (sirloin, rump, etc.)*
    2 *marrow bones (optional)*
    1 *teaspoon salt*
   10 *peppercorns*
  ½ *teaspoon thyme*
    1 *bay leaf*
    1 *tablespoon chopped parsley*
    2 *medium onions*
    4 *cloves*
    2 *stalks celery, sliced*
  ½ *pound carrots, sliced*
  ½ *pound turnips, cubed*
    2 *leeks or 6 scallions, sliced*
  ½ *pound potatoes, cubed*
    1 *small cabbage, roughly cut*
  ½ *cup red wine*
      Pickles
      Mild (Dijon) mustard
      Coarse sea salt

Place the beef, marrow bones, salt, peppercorns, thyme, bay leaf and parsley in a heavy pan. Almost cover with water, bring to a boil and skim. Reduce the heat, partially cover and simmer for 2 to 2½ hours, skimming occasionally. Spike one of the onions with the cloves and slice the other. Add these to the pot along with the celery, carrots, turnips, leeks and potatoes. Simmer, partially covered, another hour. Add the cabbage and continue simmering for ½ hour. Remove the meat and vegetables from the broth. Slice the meat and place on a platter with the vegetables. Spoon the optional marrow over slices of French bread and discard the bones. Skim any fat from the broth, add the wine and transfer to a warm bowl. Serve the meat and vegetables from the platter and pass the broth, French bread, pickles, mustard and sea salt separately.

Boeuf à la mode

Beef braised in wine

8 servings

    8 *carrots, sliced thinly*
    1 *onion, chopped finely*
    1 *bay leaf*
  ½ *teaspoon thyme*
    3 *sprigs parsley*
  ¼ *teaspoon salt*
      Freshly ground black pepper
    3 *pounds top sirloin*
 1½ *cups red wine*
    2 *tablespoons olive oil or vegetable oil*
    3 *onions, finely chopped*
    4 *cloves garlic*
   12 *large mushrooms, finely chopped*
    1 *teaspoon lemon juice*
  ½ *pound bacon*
  ½ *cup beef broth*
    3 *tablespoons flour*

Place carrots, onion, bay leaf, thyme and parsley, salt and pepper in a bowl. Add the beef and wine. Cover and marinate the beef in the refrigerator for 24 hours. Turn the beef every 8 hours. Remove the meat. Dry on paper towels. Strain and reserve the marinade. Heat the oil in a heavy casserole and brown the meat on all sides over high heat. Lower the heat and fry onions and garlic in the same oil for 3 minutes. Add mushrooms and lemon juice and continue cooking for 5 minutes. In the meantime, fry bacon until almost crisp. Drain and leave to one side. Heat reserved marinade with beef broth. Stir flour into onions and mushrooms. Add bacon. Replace beef in the casserole and stir in warm wine and broth. Cover and cook 2½ hours in a 350° oven.

Beckenoff

Pork and lamb baked with potatoes

6 servings

  2 tablespoons butter
  6 potatoes, peeled and
    sliced thinly
  2 large onions, sliced thinly
  1 teaspoon salt
    Freshly ground black pepper
1½ pounds pork tenderloin,
    trimmed and sliced thinly
1½ pounds lamb shoulder,
    trimmed and sliced thinly
  ½ teaspoon thyme
  1 bay leaf
  4 tablespoons finely chopped
    parsley
  ½ cup white wine
  ½ cup chicken broth
  1 tablespoon cornflour
    dissolved in 2 tablespoons
    cold water
  1 tablespoon butter
  2 tablespoons finely chopped
    parsley

Butter a large baking dish
with 1 tablespoon of butter.
Cover with half of the potatoes,
then arrange half of the onion
rings on top of the potatoes.
Season lightly with salt and
pepper. Place half of both
kinds of meat on top of the
onions. Season with salt and
pepper. Add thyme, bay leaf
and half of the parsley.
Add remaining meats and
season again with salt and
pepper. Add a layer of onion
rings, a layer of potatoes and
again season with salt and
pepper. Pour in wine and
chicken broth. Dot with
remaining tablespoon of butter.

Cover tightly with aluminum
foil. Bake in a 350° oven for
2 hours. Remove foil, stir in
cornflour paste and heat until
sauce is thickened. Dot surface
with butter. Brown potatoes
under the grill for 3 minutes.
Garnish with finely chopped
parsley and serve hot.

Côte de boeuf à la Bordelaise

Rib steak in Bordelaise sauce

6 servings

3½ pounds rib steak with the
    bone or 2½ pounds
    boneless sirloin steak cut
    1 inch thick
  2 tablespoons butter
  1 tablespoon olive oil or
    vegetable oil
  ½ teaspoon salt
    Freshly ground black pepper
  4 tablespoons finely chopped
    scallions
  1 clove garlic, crushed
  ½ cup red wine
  ¼ teaspoon thyme
  1 tablespoon lemon juice
  1 tablespoon brandy
  4 tablespoons butter, softened
  2 tablespoons finely chopped
    parsley
  2 tablespoons beef marrow,
    (diced and simmered in
    boiling water for 3 minutes),
    if available

Sauté steak in a heavy skillet
in combined hot butter and oil.
Adjust the heat to prevent the
butter from burning. Cook
steaks 4 to 5 minutes on each
side. Transfer to a hot plate.
Season with salt and pepper
and keep hot. Stir scallions
and garlic into the same
skillet. Sauté scallions for
three minutes. Add wine,
stirring in all the browned
juices from the bottom of the
pan. Add thyme, lemon juice
and brandy. Boil over high
heat until the wine is reduced
to about 3 tablespoons.
Remove skillet from the heat

and beat in the butter and
finely chopped parsley.
Add beef marrow if available.
Serve sauce separately.

*Pot au feu, recipe page 46,
1st column*

Choucroute Alsacienne

Choucroute Alsacienne

Jambon persillé

Sauerkraut Alsatian style

8 servings

- 3 pounds sauerkraut
- ½ teaspoon caraway seeds (optional)
- 1 tablespoon black peppercorns
- 2 cups white wine
- ½ pound bacon, thickly sliced
- 4 pork sausages
- 4 bratwurst or knackwurst
- 4 frankfurters
- 8 pork chops
- ¼ teaspoon salt
  Freshly ground black pepper
- 1 pound smoked or cooked ham, cut into small pieces
- 2 pounds potatoes, boiled

Rinse sauerkraut under cold running water and squeeze dry. Place sauerkraut in a large skillet. Add caraway seeds, peppercorns and white wine. Cover and simmer 20 minutes. Fry bacon until crisp and all the fat has rendered. Drain bacon and reserve bacon fat. Return 1 tablespoon fat to the skillet. Brown pork sausages, bratwurst and frankfurters in hot fat. Drain on paper towels. Add two more tablespoons reserved bacon fat to the skillet. Brown pork chops in hot fat for 8 minutes. Turn, season with salt and pepper and cook 8 minutes on the second side. Brown ham in the same skillet. Arrange pork chops and sausage on a bed of sauerkraut. Place in a 375° oven for ten minutes. Serve hot with boiled potatoes.

Ham in parsley and wine sauce

- 3 pounds cooked ham, cut in large cubes
- ½ teaspoon thyme
- 1 bay leaf
- ½ teaspoon salt (more or less depending on saltiness of the ham)
  Freshly ground black pepper
- 2 shallots or scallions, finely chopped
- 1 stalk celery, chopped
- 2½ cups chicken broth
- 2½ cups dry white wine
- ½ to ¾ cup finely chopped parsley
- 2 packages unflavored gelatin
- ½ cup water
- 1 to 2 tablespoons tarragon vinegar

In a large pan, place the ham, thyme, bay leaf, salt, pepper, shallots, celery, broth and white wine. Bring to a simmer, cover and cook slowly 30 minutes. Remove the ham with a slotted spoon and place in a wet serving bowl. Toss the ham with a little of the chopped parsley. Sprinkle the gelatin over the water to soften. Strain the liquid in which the ham has cooked into another pan. Add the softened gelatin and stir to dissolve, then add the vinegar and remaining parsley. Cool until the liquid starts to set and pour over the ham. Refrigerate overnight before serving.

Cassoulet

Cassoulet

12 servings

- 2 *pounds white beans*
- 3 *quarts boiling water*
- ½ *pound pork rind, if available or ¼ pound bacon, cut into small pieces*
- ½ *pound salt pork*
- 2 *onions, chopped*
- 2 *cloves garlic, crushed*
- 4 *sprigs parsley*
- 2 *bay leaves*
- 1 *teaspoon thyme*
- 4 *chicken bouillon cubes, dissolved in 1 cup boiling water*
- 3 *quarts water*
- 1 *pound Polish sausage*
- 1 *pound shoulder of lamb, cut into 2 inch cubes*
- 1 *pound pork loin, cut into 2 inch cubes*
- 3 *tablespoons olive oil or vegetable oil*
- 2 *onions, finely chopped*
- 2 *cloves garlic, crushed*
- 2 *stalks celery, chopped*
- 1 *cup white wine*
- 1 *cup beef broth*
- ½ *teaspoon salt*
- *Freshly ground black pepper*
- 4 *tomatoes peeled, seeded and chopped*
- 1 *bay leaf*
- 1 *(4½ pounds) duck*
- 1½ *cups breadcrumbs*

Rinse beans and add to a large casserole of boiling water. Boil for 5 minutes. Remove from the heat and allow beans to soak for 1 hour. Cover pork rind or bacon with 2 cups cold water. Bring to boiling point. Drain, rinse under cold water and repeat this process. Place drained beans, pork rind or bacon, salt pork, onions, garlic, parsley, bay leaves and thyme and dissolved bouillon cubes in a large casserole. Cover with cold water. Add Polish sausage. Simmer uncovered for 1½ hours. (Remove sausage after 30 minutes). Discard bay leaves. Drain beans and reserve broth. Brown lamb and pork in hot oil in a large skillet. Add onions, garlic and celery. Cook 5 minutes and add wine and broth. Season with salt and pepper and add tomatoes and bay leaf. Cover and simmer 1½ hours until meat is tender. Remove meat from the broth. Roast the duck 1¼ hours and cut into 2 inch pieces and reserve 3 tablespoons fat from duck. Place a layer of beans in a large casserole. Add a layer of ½ the sausage, sliced. Add a layer of lamb, pork and duck. Cover with more beans, another layer of the meats, then the remaining beans. Top with sausage. Add reserved bean broth. There should be enough to come almost to the top of the beans. Add chicken broth if there is not enough bean liquid. Cover with a thick layer of breadcrumbs and drizzle with reserved duck fat. Place over direct heat until the broth is simmering. Place in a 350° oven for 1 hour. This magnificently flavored casserole involves several fairly lengthy cooking procedures, but none of them are difficult and the dish can be prepared over a period of 2 days. However, it is best to assemble the dish and complete the final cooking when you are just ready to eat it. This is an extremely good and quite inexpensive party dish.

Boeuf à la Bourguignonne

Entrecôte marchand de vin

Steak au poivre

Beef Bourguignon

6 servings

  3 pounds lean boneless
      chuck, cubed
  1 large onion, thinly sliced
½ teaspoon thyme
  1 bay leaf
  1 tablespoon chopped parsley
  1 clove garlic, crushed
½ teaspoon salt
      Freshly ground black pepper
  1 cup dry red wine
  2 tablespoons olive oil
¼ pound lean salt pork
      or sliced bacon, cut into
      thin strips
18 small white onions
  2 tablespoons flour
1½ cups beef broth or bouillon
½ pound mushrooms
  2 tablespoons butter

Place the meat, onion, thyme, bay leaf, parsley, garlic, salt and pepper in a bowl. Combine the wine and olive oil, pour over the beef and marinate for 4 or more hours, stirring occasionally. Place the salt pork or bacon strips in a heavy casserole and sauté until the fat is rendered. Add the small white onions and sauté until tender and browned and the salt pork or bacon is crisp. Remove from the pan. Dry the cubes of beef well with paper towels and reserve the marinade. Sauté the beef in the hot fat, browning well on all sides. Sprinkle on the flour, cook for a few minutes and pour on the marinade and beef bouillon. Bring to a simmer, cover and cook for

2 hours or until beef is tender. In the meantime, lightly sauté the mushrooms in the butter. When the beef is done, taste for seasoning, add the salt pork or bacon, onions and mushrooms to the casserole and simmer another 15 minutes to blend the flavors. Serve from the casserole. This dish is best prepared one day before it is to be served.

Steak in red wine

4 servings

  4 fillet steaks
      (6–8 ounces each, cut
1½ inches thick)
  1 tablespoon butter
  1 tablespoon vegetable oil
½ teaspoon salt
      Freshly ground black pepper
¾ cup red wine
  4 tablespoons scallions,
      chopped
½ teaspoon thyme
  1 bay leaf
¼ teaspoon Bovril
  3 tablespoons butter, softened

Sauté steaks in hot butter and oil over high heat for 3 minutes on each side. Place on a hot serving dish. Season with salt and pepper and keep warm. In the meantime, prepare the sauce: Pour the wine into a small saucepan. Add scallions, thyme and bay leaf. Boil over high heat until reduced to ½ cup. Stir in Bovril (meat glaze) and butter. Boil 2 more minutes. Remove the bay leaf. Pour sauce over steaks and serve immediately.

Pepper steak

4 servings

  4 boneless tenderloin or
      sirloin steaks
  2 tablespoons oil
1½ tablespoons peppercorns or
      1 tablespoon cracked pepper
  4 tablespoons butter
  2 shallots or scallions,
      finely chopped
⅓ cup dry white wine
¼ cup beef broth
⅓ cup brandy

Dry the steaks well with paper towels. Rub them on both sides with 1 tablespoon oil. Crush the peppercorns and press firmly into both sides of the steaks. Let stand 1 to 2 hours. In a heavy pan, heat the remaining oil and 2 tablespoons of the butter until very hot. Sauté the steaks over high heat for about 3 minutes on each side for rare meat. Transfer them to a hot platter and sprinkle with salt. Add the shallots to the pan and sauté for a few minutes. Pour in the wine and broth and boil rapidly, scraping up the meat juices clinging to the pan. Warm the brandy, ignite it and add to the pan. When the flames have died down, remove the pan from the heat and beat in the remaining butter. Pour the sauce over the steaks and serve.

Filet de boeuf en croûte

Blanquette de veau

Beef Wellington

8 servings

- 5 *pound fillet of beef with its covering fat*
- 1 *teaspoon salt*
  Freshly ground black pepper
- 2 *tablespoons butter*
- 2 *pounds mushrooms, finely chopped*
- 6 *tablespoons scallions, finely chopped*
- 2 *tablespoons flour*
- 1 *tablespoon lemon juice*
- 1/3 *cup sherry or Madeira wine*
- 1 *(3 ounce) can liver pâté*
- 2 *packages frozen puff pastry or double recipe for pastry (page 93)*
- 1 *egg yolk*
- 2 *tablespoons milk*

Have the butcher remove the fat and tie the beef with string at 2 inch intervals. Place the beef on a roasting rack, cover with the reserved fat and roast in a 400° oven for 20 minutes. Discard the fat. Season beef with salt and pepper. Allow beef to cool. It will stiffen as it cools. Heat the butter in a skillet and simmer mushrooms and scallions for 15 minutes. Stir in the flour. Add lemon juice, and sherry. Add liver pâté. Spread mushroom mixture over the cool beef. Thaw pastry.
Form pastry into a ball and roll into a rectangle on a lightly floured board, or prepare alternative pastry. The pastry should be large enough to enclose the beef completely. Wrap beef in the pastry sheet folding the edges neatly. Place beef on a buttered and floured baking sheet. Prick the surface of the pastry to allow the steam to escape as the cooking is completed. Brush pastry with combined egg yolk and milk. Place in a 400° oven for 15 minutes. Lower the heat to 350° and continue cooking for 20 minutes until beef is rare and pastry is browned. Allow the beef to rest 15 minutes before cutting into thick slices.
Serve hot with Madeira sauce (page 27).
Note: There are four separate processes in preparing beef Wellington. The beef has a preliminary roasting; the mushroom mixture is prepared, and the pastry is made. Finally, it is all assembled and cooked. Except for the final cooking the other steps can be taken over a period of two days. This is a dramatic and expensive dish but worthy to serve for a very special occasion.

Veal stew

6 servings

- 2½ *pounds stewing veal cut from the shoulder and cut into 2 inch squares*
- 1 *onion, chopped*
- 2 *carrots, sliced*
- ½ *teaspoon salt*
- 1 *bay leaf*
- 3 *stalks parsley*
- 2 *cups water*
- 3 *tablespoons butter*
- 4 *tablespoons scallions, finely chopped*
- 6 *mushrooms, quartered*
- 3 *tablespoons flour*
- 2 *egg yolks*
- 1/3 *cup heavy cream*
- 1 *tablespoon lemon juice*
- 2 *tablespoons finely chopped parsley*

Place veal, onion, carrots, salt, bay leaf and parsley in a casserole. Add cold water and heat to simmering point. Simmer five minutes. Remove scum which rises to the surface. Cover casserole and simmer over low heat for 1½ hours. Sauté scallions in 2 tablespoons butter in a skillet. Add and brown the mushrooms. Transfer to the casserole. Add remaining tablespoon of butter to the same skillet. Stir in flour and add ¾ cup hot liquid from the casserole. Stir to form a sauce.* Combine egg yolks and cream and add to the sauce. (Do not allow the sauce to boil or the egg yolks will curdle). Stir sauce into the casserole. Allow juice to thicken. Garnish with parsley. Serve hot.

* May be prepared in advance to this point.

Gigot d'agneau à la Bretonne,
recipe page 56, 1st column

Côte de boeuf à la Bordelaise,
recipe page 47, 3rd column

Veau à la Niçoise

Veal Riviera style

6 servings

2½ pounds boneless veal roast
  2 cloves garlic, quartered
  ½ teaspoon salt
     Freshly ground black pepper
  3 tablespoons olive oil or
     vegetable oil
  3 medium sized onions, sliced
  3 large ripe tomatoes, peeled,
·   seeded and chopped
  1 tablespoon finely chopped
     parsley
  ½ teaspoon marjoram

Make deep slits in the veal and
insert garlic quarters. Brown
meat lightly in hot oil. Remove
meat from the pan. Add onions
and simmer over medium heat
for 3 minutes. Add tomatoes,
parsley and marjoram.
Season veal with salt and
pepper. Place veal on the bed
of vegetables. Roast in a 300°
oven for 1½ hours. Slice and
serve hot or cold.

Côte de veau Vallée d'Auge

Veal cutlets with mushrooms

4 servings

  4 veal cutlets, 4 ounces each,
     pounded thin
  2 tablespoons butter
  ¼ pound mushrooms, thinly
     sliced
  ¼ pound small white onions,
     blanched in boiling salted
     water for about 8 minutes
     or until tender
  ¾ cup heavy cream
  ½ teaspoon salt
     Freshly ground black pepper
  ¼ cup apple brandy
  1 teaspoon lemon juice
  1 tablespoon cornflour,
     dissolved in 2 tablespoons
     water

In a heavy skillet, heat the
butter until foaming and sauté
the cutlets for about 2 minutes
on each side. Transfer them
to a warm serving plate.
Add the mushrooms and onions
to the skillet and sauté 3
minutes until softened. Pour
on the cream. Season with salt
and pepper and simmer 3
minutes. Add the apple brandy
and simmer another 3 minutes.
Add lemon juice to taste and
thicken into a sauce with the
cornflour mixture. Pour the
sauce over the veal and
serve hot.

Filet de boeuf en croûte,
recipe page 51, 1st column

Selle d'agneau bouquetière,
recipe page 55, 3rd column

Rognons de veau aux tomates

Veal kidneys with tomatoes

4 servings

1½ pounds calves' or lamb
    kidneys
  1 onion, finely chopped
  2 tablespoons butter
  8 button mushrooms
  1 teaspoon paprika
  1 tablespoon mild (Dijon)
    mustard
1½ tablespoons flour
  1 cup beef broth
  2 tomatoes, peeled, seeded
    and chopped
 ¼ cup heavy cream
 ¼ teaspoon salt
    Freshly ground black pepper
  2 tablespoons parsley,
    finely chopped

Cut kidneys into small pieces,
cutting around white inner core.
Sauté onion in butter for 3
minutes until softened. Add
and sauté kidneys and
mushrooms for 3 minutes
over high heat. Lower the heat
and stir in paprika, mustard
and flour. Add beef broth,
tomatoes and cream. Season
with salt and pepper. Simmer
5 minutes until kidneys are
tender. Garnish with finely
chopped parsley.

Noisettes de porc aux pruneaux

Pork loin with prunes

4 servings

    1 cup dried prunes
    1 cup red wine
 1½ pounds pork loin, cut into
        thick slices or 4 thick
        pork chops
    1 tablespoon butter
    1 tablespoon olive oil
        or vegetable oil
  ½ teaspoon salt
        Freshly ground black pepper
    2 tablespoons flour
  ½ cup beef broth
    1 tablespoon red currant jelly
  ½ cup heavy cream
    2 tablespoons finely chopped
        parsley

Soak prunes in red wine for
12 hours. Simmer prunes and
wine, uncovered, in a small
saucepan for 30 minutes until
prunes are tender and the wine
has reduced slightly. Brown
pork chops in combined hot
butter and oil. Continue
cooking 6 minutes on each side.
Remove chops and season
with salt and pepper. Discard
all but 2 tablespoons of fat
in the skillet. Stir in flour.
Add beef broth and wine from
the prunes. Keep prunes warm.
Add red currant jelly and
cream. Simmer sauce five
minutes. Return chops to the
skillet and simmer 15 minutes
over low heat. Garnish with
warm prunes and chopped
parsley.

Côtelettes de porc au cidre

Pork chops in apple cider

4 servings

    4 thick pork chops
    1 tablespoon butter
    1 tablespoon olive oil or
        vegetable oil
  ½ teaspoon salt
        Freshly ground black pepper
    2 tablespoons flour
 1¼ cups apple cider
    1 clove garlic, crushed
    1 teaspoon rosemary
    1 teaspoon capers

Brown chops in combined hot
butter and oil. Cook chops
6 minutes on each side. Remove
chops from the skillet and
season with salt and pepper.
Discard all but 2 tablespoons
fat from the skillet. Stir flour
into the skillet. Add apple
cider, garlic and rosemary.
Simmer sauce 5 minutes until
thickened and slightly reduced.
Replace chops. Cover and
simmer for 15 minutes. Stir
capers into the sauce 5 minutes
before serving time. Serve hot.

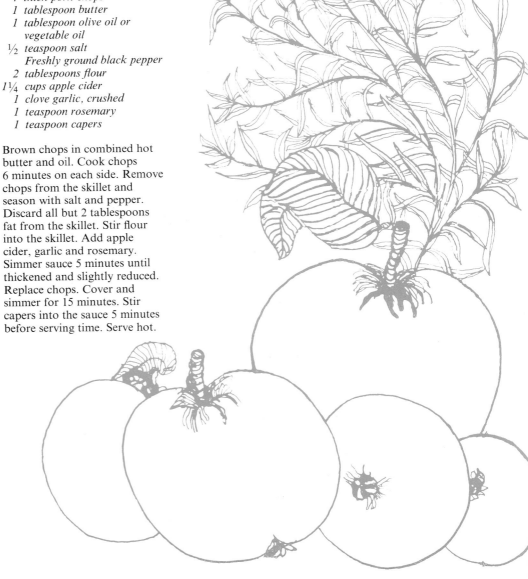

oie de veau Véronique

Calves liver with grapes

servings

6 slices calves' liver
½ cup flour seasoned with
  ½ teaspoon salt
  Freshly ground black pepper
1 tablespoon oil
2 tablespoons butter
¼ cup sweet vermouth
1 cup beef broth
¼ teaspoon thyme
½ cup white seedless grapes

redge the liver slices in the
asoned flour. Melt the butter
ad oil in a large skillet.
hen the butter is foaming,
uté the liver slices for 2
3 minutes on each side.
emove to a heated platter.
dd the vermouth, broth and
yme to the skillet. Boil over
gh heat, scraping up the
owned bits clinging to the
ottom of the pan. When the
uce has reduced to about
cup, add the grapes and
at through. Taste for
asoning. Pour the sauce over
e liver and serve hot.

Boeuf aux champignons

Beef with mushrooms

4 servings

2 pounds fillet of beef
1 tablespoon butter
1 tablespoon olive oil or
  vegetable oil
1 onion, finely chopped
1 clove garlic, crushed
4 mushrooms, thinly sliced
2 tablespoons flour
1 teaspoon tomato paste
½ cup red wine
¾ cup beef broth
½ teaspoon salt
  Freshly ground black pepper
½ teaspoon thyme
2 tablespoons parsley,
  finely chopped

Cut beef into thin slices and
then into strips. Sauté beef
strips in a skillet in combined
butter and oil over high heat
for 5 minutes. Stir beef to
prevent it from sticking. Stir
in onion and garlic. Cook 3
minutes. Add mushrooms and
cook 2 minutes. Fold in flour
and tomato paste. Stir in wine
and beef broth. Season with
salt and pepper. Add thyme
and simmer 3 more minutes.
Garnish with parsley. Serve hot.

Selle d'agneau bouquetière

Roast lamb with garden vegetables

8 servings

6 pound leg or shoulder
  of lamb
2 cloves garlic, slivered
1 teaspoon thyme
1 teaspoon salt
  Freshly ground black pepper
  Juice of 1 lemon
2 tablespoons olive oil
1 cauliflower
2 pounds green beans
1 pound asparagus
1 pound new potatoes
¼ cup butter
8 small tomatoes
8 medium sized mushroom
  caps
2 tablespoons butter
¼ teaspoon salt
  Freshly ground black pepper
1 bunch watercress, washed
  and thoroughly dried

Make slits in the roast and
insert garlic slivers. Sprinkle
with thyme, salt and pepper
and rub with lemon juice and
olive oil. Place the meat in a
roasting pan and cook
uncovered in a 450° oven for
15 to 20 minutes or until nicely
browned. Reduce the heat to
350°, insert a meat thermometer
and roast, basting occasionally
with the pan drippings, until
the meat reaches the desired
degree of doneness. The total
time will be 10 to 12 minutes
per pound for medium rare,
which is the preference in
France, or 13 to 15 minutes
per pound for well done.
In the meantime, prepare the
vegetables, dividing the
cauliflower into sections. Cook
the cauliflower, green beans,
and asparagus separately in
boiling salted water until tender
but still firm. If frozen
vegetables are used, follow the
package directions. Canned
vegetables should simply be
heated through. Boil the
potatoes, covered, until not
quite done, then sauté in the
butter until golden. Blanch
the whole tomatoes in boiling
water for 2 to 3 minutes,
making sure they remain firm.
Remove the cores and slip off
the skins. Sauté the mushroom
caps in 2 tablespoons butter
for 3 to 5 minutes and season
with salt and pepper. When the
roast is done, place on a
warmed platter and surround
with the vegetables. Garnish
with watercress and serve.

Gigot d'agneau à la Bretonne

Leg of Lamb Brittany style

6 to 8 servings

6 pound leg of lamb, boned
   and tied
2 cloves garlic, slivered
4 tablespoons olive oil
1 teaspoon salt
   Freshly ground black pepper
1 teaspoon rosemary
1 cup dry white wine
1 cup beef broth
1 pound white beans,
   soaked overnight if necessary
1 medium sized onion, quartered
1 bay leaf
1 teaspoon salt
   Freshly ground black pepper
1 tablespoon butter
   Finely chopped parsley for
   garnish

Make slits in the roast and insert garlic slivers. Heat the oil in a large, heavy casserole and brown the roast on all sides. Pour out the oil and add the salt, pepper, rosemary, white wine and beef broth to the pan with the lamb. Bring to a simmer, cover and cook slowly on top of the stove or in a 300° oven for 2½ to 3 hours or until tender. While the lamb is cooking, place the beans, onion, bay leaf, salt and pepper in a heavy saucepan. Cover with water, bring to a boil, cover and simmer 1½ to 2 hours or until tender. When the lamb is done, remove it from the casserole and keep warm. Skim the fat from the liquid and boil it down to concentrate the flavor. Drain the beans, stir in 2 tablespoons of the reduced liquid and transfer to an ovenproof serving dish.

Slice the lamb and arrange attractively on top of the beans. Moisten with a little of the liquid, dot with butter and place in a 400° oven for 4 minutes. Garnish with chopped parsley before serving. Pass the remaining braising liquid separately.

Navarin de mouton

Lamb stew

6 servings

2½ pounds shoulder of lamb,
   cut into 3 inch cubes
1 tablespoon butter
2 tablespoons vegetable oil
3 onions, sliced
2 cloves garlic, crushed
2 tablespoons flour
1½ cups beef broth
½ teaspoon salt
   Freshly ground black pepper
1 teaspoon rosemary
1 bay leaf
12 small potatoes, peeled
6 carrots, sliced
½ turnip (optional), chopped
1½ pounds fresh peas in the pod
   or 1 package frozen peas

Brown lamb in hot butter and oil. Transfer lamb to a casserole. Sauté onions and garlic in the same skillet. Stir in flour and add beef broth. Season with salt and pepper. Add rosemary and bay leaf. Add these ingredients to the lamb. Bring broth to boiling point. Lower heat, cover and simmer for 1 hour until lamb is almost tender. Add potatoes, carrots and turnip and simmer for 20 minutes. Add peas and continue simmering another 10 minutes. Serve hot.

Côtelettes de mouton Comtoise

Broiled lamb chops in onion sauce

4 servings

8 loin lamb chops
2 tablespoons olive oil or
   vegetable oil
½ teaspoon salt
   Freshly ground black pepper
8 medium sized onions, sliced
2 cloves garlic, crushed
2 tablespoons butter
2 tablespoons flour
⅓ cup heavy cream

Heat butter and simmer onions and garlic over moderate heat for 30 minutes until a soft purée is formed. Stir in flour and add cream. Simmer another 15 minutes. Brush lamb chops with oil and broil 8 minutes on each side. Season with salt and pepper. Place onion purée on a hot serving plate. Arrange lamb on the purée and serve hot.

Coq au vin,
recipe page 62, 1st column

Canard aux pruneaux

Duck with prunes

4 servings

  1 *(4½ to 5 pound) duckling*
  ½ *teaspoon salt*
      Freshly ground black pepper
  ½ *pound dried pitted prunes*
  ½ *cup port wine*
  2 *teaspoons lemon juice*
  4 *tablespoons sugar*
1½ *cups duck stock or beef broth*
  3 *tablespoons of wine vinegar*
  2 *tablespoons arrowroot or*
      cornflour dissolved in 3
      tablespoons port wine

Season the cavity of the duck with salt and pepper. Prick the skin of the duck and place on a rack in a roasting pan. Roast in a 325° oven for 1½ hours. Prick the skin occasionally and remove excess fat from the pan. In the meantime, combine the prunes, ¼ cup port wine, lemon juice and 2 tablespoons of sugar in a bowl. Let stand until the duck is cooked. Remove the duck to a warmed platter. Pour the fat out of the roasting pan, add the bouillon and boil over high heat scraping up the brown pieces clinging to the pan. Transfer the liquid to a heavy saucepan, add the remaining port, sugar, wine vinegar and prune mixture. Simmer for 10 minutes. Remove the prunes with a slotted spoon and arrange around the duck. Thicken the sauce with the arrowroot mixture and spoon a little over the duck. Serve the rest in a separate bowl.

Canards à l'orange en gelée

Duck with orange in aspic

8 servings

- 2 (4 pound) ducks
- 5 oranges
- 2 teaspoons salt
  Freshly ground black pepper
- 2 tablespoons butter, melted
- 1 tablespoon oil
- ½ cup sherry or Madeira wine
- 3 cups chicken broth
- 2 packages (2 tablespoons) unflavored gelatin dissolved in ⅓ cup cold water
- 8 individual prepared pastry shells
- 40 thin fresh asparagus tips, cooked or 2 packages frozen peas, cooked
- 16 black cherries in heavy syrup, drained

Peel 2 oranges, cut them into quarters and stuff the ducks. Season the cavity with salt and pepper. Truss ducks. Prick the skin with a fork and place on a rack in large roasting pan. Brush duck with combined oil and butter. Roast uncovered in a 350° oven for 1¼ hours. Chill the ducks. Heat wine and chicken broth in a saucepan. Pour ⅓ cup cold water into a small cup. Sprinkle gelatin powder on top of the water and allow it to stand undisturbed for 5 minutes. Add gelatin to simmering broth and stir to dissolve. Chill the broth until it is just beginning to set, about 1 hour. Pour a thin layer of wine jelly into a large serving tray. Chill and allow it to set firmly. Place ducks on the tray and brush with half-set jelly.

(If the jelly becomes too firm, heat it slightly.) Allow jelly to set until firm. Peel one orange. Cut the peel into thin strips and simmer in a saucepan of boiling water for ten minutes. Drain peel and allow it to cool. Cut remaining two oranges into slices. Garnish tray with orange slices, cherries and poached orange peel. Spoon remaining jelly over the ducks and chill until serving time. Fill pastry with asparagus tips or peas and arrange on the tray.

Canard Montmorency

Duck with cherries

4 servings

- 1 (4 pound) duck
- ½ teaspoon salt
  Freshly ground black pepper
- 2 small whole onions, peeled
- 4 cloves
- 1½ cups chicken broth
- ¼ teaspoon thyme
- 1 bay leaf
- 1 teaspoon salt
- ½ cup red port wine or other sweet red wine
- 1 tablespoon lemon juice
- 1 (1 pound) jar black pitted cherries, drained
- 2 packages (2 tablespoons) unflavored gelatin

Place ½ teaspoon salt, pepper and onions stuck with 4 cloves inside the duck cavity. Put the duck in a casserole. Add giblets except the liver. Add chicken broth, thyme, bay leaf and salt. Cover and simmer slowly for 1½ hours. Remove duck and discard the onions. Chill in the refrigerator. Strain the broth and chill for 4 hours. Skim off the fat from the broth. Boil broth until reduced to 1 cup. Place broth, wine, lemon juice and ½ cup drained cherry juice in a saucepan. Sprinkle the gelatin on the liquid and allow to stand undisturbed for 5 minutes. Heat over gentle heat until gelatin is dissolved. Do not allow it to boil. Chill broth in a bowl until set. Unmold jelly and chop on a board with a knife. Place the cold duck on a serving platter. Garnish with drained cherries and serve the chopped jelly separately.

Poulet en cocotte de grandmère

Hens or game hens with red wine

4 servings

- 4 *hens*
- 4 *tablespoons butter*
- 1 *tablespoon olive oil or vegetable oil*
- ½ *pound bacon, fried until crisp and drained*
- 2 *onions, finely chopped*
- 1 *clove garlic, crushed*
- 4 *mushrooms, sliced thinly*
- 2 *tablespoons flour*
- 1 *cup beef broth*
- ½ *cup red wine*
- 1 *bay leaf*
- ½ *teaspoon thyme*
- 3 *tablespoons finely chopped parsley*
- 1 *teaspoon salt*
  Freshly ground black pepper

Brown hens lightly in 2 tablespoons of butter and oil. Transfer hens to a large casserole. Add drained and crumbled bacon. Sauté onions and garlic in the same butter for 3 minutes. Add and sauté mushrooms until lightly browned. Stir in the flour and add beef broth and wine. Pour into the casserole and add the bay leaf, thyme and 1 tablespoon of parsley. Season with salt and pepper. Cover and cook in a 350° oven for 45 minutes. Garnish with remaining parsley. Serve with glazed onions, (see page 71) and freshly boiled new potatoes.
This dish, rich and full of flavor can also be prepared with partridge, quail, dove and other game birds in the hunting season.

Pintadeaux farcis

Stuffed guinea hen

4 servings

- 4 *guinea hens with the livers*
- 4 *tablespoons butter*
- 4 *shallots or scallions, finely chopped*
- ½ *pound cottage cheese*
- 4 *tablespoons fine dry breadcrumbs*
- ½ *teaspoon salt*
  Freshly ground black pepper
  Dash of nutmeg
- ½ *teaspoon ground cloves*
- ¼ *teaspoon thyme*
- 1 *tablespoon finely chopped parsley*
- ¾ *cup dry sherry*
- 2 *tablespoons olive oil*
- 1 *cup chicken broth*
- 2 *bay leaves*
- ¼ *teaspoon salt*
- 3 *tablespoons heavy cream*
- 2 *teaspoons cornflour, dissolved in 2 tablespoons water*
- 4 *slices thin white bread, crusts removed, and browned in butter*

Wash the hens and dry thoroughly. Heat 2 tablespoons of the butter in a heavy skillet and sauté the livers about five minutes. Add the shallots and cook until lightly browned. Remove the livers, cool and chop finely. Combine the shallots, livers, cottage cheese, bread crumbs, salt, pepper, nutmeg, cloves, thyme, parsley and 1 tablespoon of the sherry and mix thoroughly. Stuff the hens with this mixture. Do not pack the stuffing tightly. Close the opening with skewers. In a heavy casserole that is just large enough for the 4 hens, melt remaining butter and olive oil until sizzling. Brown the hens 2 at a time on all sides. Pour out the browning oil, return the birds to the pan and add remaining sherry, chicken broth, bay leaves and ¼ teaspoon salt. Bring to a simmer, drape wax paper over the birds, cover the pan and cook slowly about 45 minutes or until tender. Remove the skewers and transfer the hens to a warm serving platter, placing each on top of a slice of browned bread. Discard the bay leaves from the sauce. Boil rapidly, skimming off any fat. Add the cream and continue to boil until slightly syrupy. Thicken, if desired with the cornstarch mixture. Moisten the hens with a little of the sauce and pass the remainder separately. Garnish the platter with watercress and serve.

It may be more than a
coincidence that the rooster is the
French national symbol since in
many ways the chicken is the
symbol of French cooking.
Napoleon's cook once wagered
that he could set a different
chicken dish on the table for each
of the 365 days of the year. He
won the bet hands down. When
the 365 days were over, he had
not come close to using up his
inventiveness and imagination.
Another convinced Frenchman
saw the chicken playing a role in
the art of cooking like the canvas
in the art of painting. It was, he
wrote, a source of inspiration
from which one can create
anything.
To begin with, a French chicken
is never simply a chicken.
Chickens are distinguished
according to their place of origin.
There are common chickens
(which come from anywhere in
France, but are always fed on
corn) and superfine chickens
which come from the region of
Bresse in eastern France and
always carry a small lead seal on
the leg to designate the place of
origin (just as a bottle of wine
carries a label). Secondly, a
chicken is distinguished
according to its age: a
spring-chicken must not weigh
more than three-quarters of a
pound and is mostly eaten in
autumn either roasted or stuffed.
A roaster is a little older and
must not weigh more than two
pounds: it is mostly roasted or
broiled and used in delicious

recipes with refined sauces. Next
comes the large, mature hen with
white, tender flesh which is
usually first braised and then
stewed or poached in white wine
and herbs. The hen often ends up
beautifully garnished on a buffet
table. Last of all comes the old
rooster who has seen a lot in his
well-spent life and finds a worthy
end (at least from the cook's
point of view) in the soup pot.
Using an old rooster for this
purpose is not an instance of the
Frenchman's proverbial
thriftiness (they are never thrifty
when it comes to food), the point
is that only an old rooster
toughened by an adventurous life
can give real body and substance
to the broth.

Canards à l'orange en gelée,
recipe page 58, 1st column

Poule au pot

Chicken in the pot

6 servings

    1 *(4 to 5 pound) chicken*
  ½ *pound carrots, cut into*
        thick chunks
    3 *leeks, white part only, or*
        6 scallions, sliced
    2 *stalks celery, roughly cut*
    2 *turnips, roughly cut*
    2 *large onions, quartered*
    4 *cloves*
    2 *teaspoons salt*
        Freshly ground black pepper
  ½ *teaspoon thyme*
    1 *bay leaf*
    1 *tablespoon chopped parsley*
    2 *cloves garlic, crushed*

Place all the ingredients in a
large pot and cover with water.
Bring to a boil and skim the
broth. Lower the heat, cover and
simmer 1 to 1½ hours. Carve
the chicken and place it on a
serving platter surrounded by
the vegetables. Strain the broth
and serve separately as a soup.

Coq au vin

Chicken in wine sauce

6 servings

¼ pound lean salt pork or sliced
    bacon, cut into thin strips
¼ pound carrots, sliced
18 small white onions
 2 medium sized tomatoes,
    peeled, seeded and sliced
 2 (2½ pound) chickens, cut
    into serving pieces
 1 teaspoon salt
    Freshly ground black pepper
 2 tablespoons brandy, warmed
 3 tablespoons flour
 3 cups red wine
½ teaspoon thyme
 1 bay leaf
 1 tablespoon finely chopped
    parsley
½ pound mushrooms,
    quartered if large

In a large, heavy casserole,
sauté the salt pork or bacon
strips until the fat is rendered.
Add the carrots and onions and
sauté until the onions take on
color, about 5 minutes. With a
slotted spoon, remove the salt
pork and vegetables to a side
dish. Dry the pieces of chicken
thoroughly with paper towels
and sauté a few at a time in the
hot fat until golden. Sprinkle
with the salt and pepper. Ignite
the brandy and pour over the
chicken. When the flames die, add
the tomatoes and cook 3 minutes.
Return the salt pork, carrots
and onions to the casserole.
Sprinkle on the flour, stir, cook
for a few minutes and add the
wine. Bring to a boil, reduce the
heat, add the thyme, bay leaf,
parsley and mushrooms, cover

and simmer for 30 minutes or
until the chicken is tender.
Serve hot from the casserole.

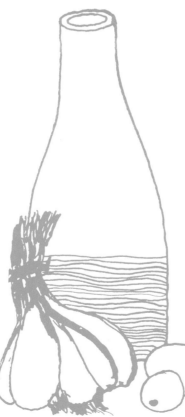

Poulet aux olives

Chicken with olives

4 servings

 2 (1½ pound) chickens, cut
    into serving pieces
 3 tablespoons olive oil or
    vegetable oil
 2 onions, finely chopped
 2 cloves garlic, crushed
 2 tablespoons flour
½ cup white wine
¼ cup white vermouth
½ cup chicken broth
 1 tablespoon tomato paste
 2 tomatoes, peeled, seeded
    and chopped
½ teaspoon salt
    Freshly ground black pepper
 1 bay leaf
½ teaspoon marjoram or oregano
 8 green olives, pitted
 8 black olives, pitted

Brown chicken in hot oil and
transfer to a casserole. Sauté
onions and garlic in the same oil.
Stir in the flour and add the
wine, vermouth and chicken
broth. Add tomato paste and
tomatoes. Season with salt and
pepper. Add marjoram and bay
leaf. Cover and cook in a 350°
oven for 50 minutes. Garnish
with black and green olives.

Poule au thym

Chicken with thyme

4 servings

 2 (1½ to 2 pound) fryers,
    halved
 1 to 2 tablespoons dried thyme
 1 tablespoon finely chopped
    parsley
 1 teaspoon salt
    Freshly ground black pepper
⅓ cup oil
¼ cup lemon juice
 1 clove garlic, crushed

Dry the chicken halves well
with paper towels. Sprinkle
them on both sides with thyme,
parsley, salt and pepper. In a
small bowl, combine the oil,
lemon juice and garlic. Grill the
chickens about 6 inches from
the flame, skin side down, for
20 minutes. Brush frequently
with the oil mixture. Turn the
chickens and grill another 20
minutes, still brushing them
with the oil. Serve hot or cold.

Poulet braisé en cocotte

Poulet à la Basquaise

Poulet à l'estragon

Braised chicken in white wine

4 servings

  2 (1½ pound) chickens cut
     into serving pieces
  2 tablespoons butter
  1 tablespoon olive oil or
     vegetable oil
  ½ pound sliced boiled ham,
     diced
  1 onion, finely chopped
  1 clove garlic, crushed
  1 green pepper, finely chopped
1½ tablespoons flour
  ½ cup white wine
  ½ cup chicken broth
  2 ripe tomatoes, peeled,
     seeded and chopped
  ½ teaspoon salt
     Freshly ground black pepper
  ½ teaspoon basil or marjoram
  2 tablespoons finely chopped
     parsley

Brown chicken pieces in hot
combined butter and oil. Transfer
chicken to a casserole. Add ham
to the casserole. Sauté onion,
garlic and green pepper in the
same butter and oil for
3 minutes. Stir in flour and add
wine, chicken broth and
tomatoes. Transfer all these
ingredients to the casserole.
Season with salt and pepper.
Cover and cook 1 hour in a 300°
oven. Add basil in the last ten
minutes of the cooking time.
Garnish with parsley and serve
with rice.

Basque chicken

4–6 servings

  1 (3½ to 4 pound) chicken
  3 tablespoons bacon fat or oil
  1 medium onion, thinly sliced
  ½ teaspoon thyme
  1 bay leaf
  ½ teaspoon salt
     Freshly ground black pepper
  1 slice orange peel
  2 cups chicken broth
  ½ pound sausages
  3 green peppers, seeded and
     cut into strips
  3 medium sized tomatoes,
     peeled, seeded and sliced
  ½ teaspoon marjoram
  ½ teaspoon salt
  1 tablespoon paprika
  1 cup rice

In a casserole just large enough
to hold the chicken, heat the
bacon fat or oil and brown the
chicken on all sides. Discard
the fat and add the onion,
thyme, bay leaf, salt, pepper,
orange peel and broth. Bring to
a simmer, cover and cook 45
minutes or until the chicken is
tender. Meanwhile, brown the
sausages in a large skillet. Drain
on paper towels and slice.
Pour off all but 2 tablespoons
of sausage fat, or add oil if there
is less than 2 tablespoons and
sauté the peppers until softened.
Add the tomatoes, marjoram
and salt and cook about 5
minutes. Sprinkle on the paprika
and cook 2 minutes more.
Remove the chicken from the
casserole, cut in serving pieces
and wrap in foil. Keep warm in
an oven heated to the lowest
possible temperature. Strain the
broth from the casserole and add
water to make 2½ cups. Bring
to a boil in a saucepan, add the
rice, and stir once with a fork.
Lower the heat, cover and simmer
slowly for 25 minutes or until
the broth is absorbed. Reheat
the pepper mixture and the
sausage in the same pan. Place
the rice on a warmed serving
dish. Arrange the chicken
pieces attractively on top and
garnish with the peppers and
sausages.

Chicken tarragon

4 servings

  1 (3 pound) chicken
  1 tablespoon butter
  ½ teaspoon salt
     Freshly ground black pepper
  1 teaspoon dried tarragon
  2 tablespoons butter
  2 carrots, diced
  1 medium sized onion, finely
     chopped
  ½ cup chicken broth
  ½ teaspoon dried tarragon
  1 tablespoon cornflour,
     dissolved in 2 tablespoons
     water

Place the 1 tablespoon of butter
in the cavity of the chicken.
Sprinkle in the salt, pepper and
tarragon and truss the chicken.
Heat 2 tablespoons of butter in
a heavy casserole until foaming
and brown the chicken on all
sides. Remove it from the pan
and set aside. If the butter is
too brown, discard it and melt
another 2 tablespoons of butter
in the casserole. Add the carrots
and onion and cook until
softened. Replace the chicken
in the casserole on the bed of
vegetables. Add the broth and
½ teaspoon of tarragon. Cover
with aluminum foil, then a lid
and simmer slowly on top of
the stove or in a 350° oven for
50 minutes or until chicken is
tender. Cut the chicken into
serving pieces and place on a
warmed platter. Thicken the pan
juices with the cornflour
mixture. Pour the sauce with
the vegetables over the chicken
and serve hot.

Coq au vin blanc

Chicken in white wine

4 servings

1 (3½ pound) chicken, cut
  into serving pieces
2 tablespoons butter
1 tablespoon olive oil or
  vegetable oil
1 onion, finely chopped
1 clove garlic, crushed
3 tablespoons flour
1 cup white wine
1 cup chicken broth
1 tablespoon tomato paste
2 ripe tomatoes, peeled, seeded
  and chopped
½ teaspoon basil
1 bay leaf
¼ teaspoon salt
  Freshly ground black pepper
2 tablespoons parsley, finely
  chopped

Brown chicken in combined
butter and oil. Transfer chicken
pieces to a casserole. In the
same skillet, sauté onion and
garlic for 3 minutes until
softened. Stir in flour and add
wine and chicken broth gradually.
Add tomato paste, tomatoes,
basil, bay leaf, salt and pepper.
Cover casserole and cook 45
minutes in a 350° oven. Garnish
with parsley.

Poulet Provençal

Provençal chicken

4 servings

- 1 *(2½ to 3 pound) chicken*
- 1 *teaspoon salt*
  Freshly ground black pepper
- 1 *teaspoon butter*
- 2 *tablespoons olive oil*
- 4 *cloves garlic, peeled and*
  cut in half
- ¼ *teaspoon rosemary*
- ½ *teaspoon basil*
- ¼ *teaspoon thyme*

Season the cavity of the chicken
with ½ teaspoon of the salt, the
pepper and butter. In a pan just
large enough to hold the chicken,
pour in 1 tablespoon of the oil
and add the garlic. Place the
chicken in the pan and sprinkle
it with the remaining salt,
pepper, rosemary, basil, thyme
and remaining olive oil. Roast
the chicken in a 425° oven for
1 hour, basting frequently.
Remove from the pan and cut
in serving pieces. Serve hot
or cold.

Salpicon de dinde à la Berrichonne

Turkey in red wine sauce

6 servings

- 3 *cups left over roast turkey,*
  cut into small pieces
- ½ *pound bacon, fried until*
  crisp, then crumbled
- 2 *tablespoons butter*
- 1 *onion, finely chopped*
- ½ *pound mushrooms, sliced*
- 1 *teaspoon paprika*
- 2 *tablespoons flour*
- 1 *cup chicken broth*
- 1 *cup red wine*
- 2 *tablespoons brandy (optional)*
- 1 *bay leaf*
- ½ *teaspoon marjoram or oregano*
- 1 *teaspoon salt*
  Freshly ground black pepper
- 2 *tablespoons finely chopped*
  parsley

Sauté onion in hot butter for
three minutes until softened.
Add mushrooms and cook over
moderate heat for 2 minutes.
Stir in the paprika and flour and
add chicken broth, red wine and
brandy. Place turkey and bacon
in a buttered baking dish.
Add bay leaf, marjoram, salt
and pepper. Add the sauce.
Cover and cook in a 400° oven
for 15 minutes. Garnish with
parsley.

Poulet au citron

Chicken with lemon

6 servings

2 *(2 pound) chickens, cut into*
  serving pieces
2 *tablespoons butter*
1 *tablespoon olive oil or*
  vegetable oil
  Grated rind and juice of
  2 lemons
1 *teaspoon salt*
  Freshly ground black pepper
2 *tablespoons finely chopped*
  parsley
2 *tablespoons finely chopped*
  chives
1 *teaspoon marjoram*
1 *tablespoon paprika*
2 *tablespoons butter*
1 *cup chicken broth*
¼ *cup white vermouth*
2 *tablespoons cornflour,*
  dissolved in 3 tablespoons
  cold water
  Watercress or parsley
  for garnish

Brown chicken pieces in combined
hot butter and oil. Adjust the
heat to prevent the butter from
burning. Transfer chicken with
its cooking butter to a large
baking dish. Sprinkle with lemon
rind and juice. Season with salt
and pepper. Cover the dish
with foil and bake in a 350° oven
for 45 minutes. Remove foil and
add parsley, chives, marjoram
and paprika. Dot chicken with
butter and place under a broiler
for 5 minutes until the skin is
crisp and golden. Pour juices
out of the dish into a saucepan.
Add chicken broth and vermouth.
Bring to boiling point and stir
in cornflour dissolved in cold
water. Simmer 2 more minutes
until sauce is thickened. Serve
hot with rice. Garnish plate with
watercress or parsley clusters.

Poulet à la moutarde

Broiled chicken with mustard

4 servings

2 *(1½ pound) frying chickens,*
  cut into quarters
2 *tablespoons butter, melted*
1 *tablespoon olive oil or*
  vegetable oil
1 *teaspoon salt*
  Freshly ground black pepper
2 *tablespoons scallions, finely*
  chopped
2 *tablespoons mild (Dijon)*
  mustard
1½ *tablespoons flour*
1 *cup chicken broth*
1 *teaspoon tomato paste*
1 *tablespoon lemon juice*
¼ *teaspoon thyme*

Brush chickens with combined
butter and oil. Season with salt
and pepper. Place 5 inches
from the broiler and grill
chickens 20 minutes on each side.
Spoon 2 tablespoons of butter
from the grill pan into a saucepan
and sauté scallions four minutes
until tender. Stir in mustard
and flour. Add chicken broth,
tomato paste, lemon juice and
thyme. Spoon sauce over the
chicken and serve hot.

Suprèmes de volaille au fromage

Chicken breasts with ham and cheese

6 servings

6 *whole (12 single breasts)*
  chicken breasts
6 *slices Proscuitto ham or*
  thinly sliced boiled ham
6 *thin slices Swiss or Gruyère*
  cheese
1 *cup flour seasoned with 1*
  teaspoon salt
  Freshly ground black pepper
3 *eggs, lightly beaten*
1 *cup fine breadcrumbs*
2 *tablespoons butter*
1 *tablespoon olive oil or*
  vegetable oil
3 *tablespoons finely chopped*
  parsley

Ask the butcher to remove skin
and bones from each chicken
breast and pound them ½ inch
thick. Cut each slice of ham and
cheese in half and place on
each breast. Fold each breast in
half. Trim ham and cheese so
they fit neatly into each breast
and do not protrude from the
edges. Dip breasts first in seasoned
flour, then into the egg and
finally into the breadcrumbs.
Heat butter and oil in a large
skillet. Sauté breasts 6 minutes on
each side until white and tender.
Garnish with parsley and
serve hot.

Poulet ou oie farcie aux pommes

Stuffed chicken or goose with apples

6 servings

1 (5 pound) roasting chicken
  or goose
2 tablespoons butter, melted
1 pound pork sausage meat
2 tablespoons butter
2 onions, finely chopped
2 stalks celery, chopped
½ cup English walnuts, chopped
2 apples, peeled, cored and
  thinly sliced
1 teaspoon salt
  Freshly ground black pepper
1 teaspoon sage
1 egg, lightly beaten
1 (1 pound) jar small unpeeled
  red apples, drained
2 pounds fresh chestnuts, boiled
  and peeled or 1 pound
  canned chestnuts

Cook pork sausage and drain off the accumulated fat. Heat 2 tablespoons butter in a skillet and sauté onions, celery and nuts for three minutes. Add and cook apples three minutes until slightly softened. Remove from the heat and stir in sausage meat. Season with salt, pepper and sage. Stir in the egg. Fill dressing into the chicken or goose and skewer the cavity. Brush chicken with melted butter. Place on a roasting rack and roast uncovered in a 375° oven for 2¼ hours. Simmer cooked chestnuts in boiling water for 5 minutes until they are hot. Place chicken or goose on a serving platter. Arrange apples and chestnuts around the chicken and serve hot.

Dinde à la Poitevine

Turkey from Poitou

6 servings

1 (4½ pound) turkey breast,
  boned, rolled and tied
3 tablespoons butter
2 medium onions, sliced
2 cloves garlic, crushed
2 slices bacon
4 medium tomatoes, peeled,
  seeded and chopped
1 teaspoon salt
  Freshly ground black pepper
½ teaspoon thyme
1 tablespoon chopped parsley
2 cups dry white wine
2 tablespoons olive oil
1 pound small white onions
1 tablespoon sugar
¼ cup dry red wine
¼ cup brandy
1 tablespoon arrowroot or
  cornflour dissolved in
  3 tablespoons water
  Sprigs of parsley

In a large heavy casserole, melt the butter until foaming. Brown the turkey quickly on all sides. Remove to a side dish and add the onions and garlic to the pan. Cook until softened. Strain off the butter. Return the turkey to the casserole and cover with bacon to prevent it from drying out. Add the tomatoes, salt, pepper, thyme, parsley and white wine. Bring to a simmer, cover and cook slowly for 2 hours or until the meat is tender Meanwhile, sauté the white onions in olive oil until golden. Drain off the oil and add the sugar and red wine. Cook until the liquid is syrupy. When the turkey is done, remove it from the casserole, wrap in aluminum foil and keep warm in a 200° oven. Strain the sauce and skim off the fat. Purée the onions and tomatoes in the blender or force through a sieve. Return the purée to the sauce and bring to a simmer. Add the white onions and brandy and simmer slowly 5 minutes. Thicken, with the arrowroot mixture. Slice the turkey and arrange attractively on a warmed platter. Pour the sauce over and decorate the dish with sprigs of parsley. Serve hot.

Poulet ou oie aux pommes,
recipe page 67, 1st column

Canard   Montmorency,
recipe page 58, 3rd column

Poulet Normande

Chicken Normandy style

4 servings

1 (3½ pound) chicken cut
  into serving pieces
4 tablespoons butter
1 tablespoon olive oil or
  vegetable oil
½ cup applejack or apple
  brandy, warmed
¼ teaspoon salt
  Freshly ground black pepper
4 large cooking apples, peeled,
  cored and thinly sliced
2 tablespoons flour
½ cup heavy cream
½ cup apple cider

Brown chicken in 2 tablespoons
butter and oil. Flame applejack
with a match and pour the
flames over the chicken. Remove
chicken from the heat and season
with salt and pepper. Cook
apples in another skillet in
remaining 2 tablespoons of butter
for 5 minutes until slightly
softened. Place apples in a baking
dish. Cover apples with chicken.
Stir flour into the skillet in which
chicken was cooked. Add cream
and cider. Simmer 5 minutes.
Spoon sauce over the chicken.
Cover with aluminum foil and
bake 40 minutes in a 350° oven.

Gratin dauphinois

Potatoes with cream and cheese

6 servings

2½ cups heavy cream
  2 tablespoons butter
  1 clove garlic, crushed
    Dash nutmeg
  6 potatoes, peeled and
    thinly sliced
 ½ cup Swiss cheese, grated
 ¼ cup Parmesan cheese, grated
 ½ teaspoon salt
    Freshly ground black pepper

Place cream, butter, garlic and nutmeg in a small saucepan. Simmer over low heat for 10 minutes until cream is reduced to 2 cups and has thickened slightly. Butter a small casserole and arrange a layer of one third of the potatoes in the bottom of the dish. Add a third of the combined cheeses, season with salt and pepper and repeat to form 3 layers. Dot with butter. Add cream. There should be enough cream to cover the potatoes. Cover casserole and cook in a 300° oven for 1 hour. Serve with roast lamb.

Chou au marrons

Braised cabbage with chestnuts

6 servings

- *1 medium sized head white cabbage*
- *1 cup chicken broth*
- *1 cup dry white wine*
- *½ teaspoon salt*
- *4 thin slices cooked ham, diced*
- *10 canned chestnuts, drained and chopped*

Wash and shred the cabbage. Plunge it into boiling salted water and cook for 2 minutes. Drain and transfer to a heavy saucepan. Add broth, white wine and salt. Bring the liquid to a boil, lower the heat, cover and cook slowly 30 to 45 minutes. Before serving, stir in the ham and chestnuts.

Ratatouille

Vegetable stew

8 servings

- *1 medium sized aubergine*
- *1 tablespoon salt*
- *¼ cup olive oil or vegetable oil*
- *2 large onions, cut into rings*
- *3 cloves garlic, crushed*
- *2 green peppers, cut into strips*
- *4 medium sized courgettes cut into bite-sized pieces*
- *2 medium sized ripe tomatoes, cut into wedges*
- *¼ teaspoon salt*
  Freshly ground black pepper
- *½ teaspoon thyme*
- *1 bay leaf*
- *2 tablespoons parsley, finely chopped*

Cut aubergine into thick slices and then into small pieces. Sprinkle with salt. Allow eggplant to stand for 30 minutes, then rinse and pat dry on paper towels. Heat the oil in a large skillet. Sauté onions and garlic for two minutes. Add green pepper and cook for two minutes. Add aubergine and cook over high heat for three minutes, stirring constantly. Add courgettes and continue stirring for three minutes. Add tomatoes, salt, pepper, thyme and bay leaf. Simmer uncovered for 40 minutes until all the vegetables are tender. Remove bay leaf.*
Garnish with parsley and serve hot.
*Can be prepared in advance to this point.
Ratatouille can also be served cold as an appetizer.

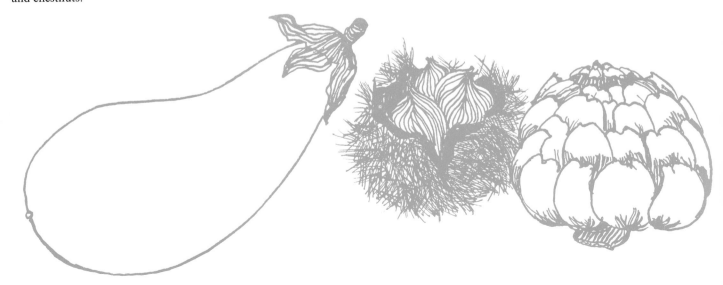

.e truffade

'ried potatoes with cheese

to 3 servings

- *1 pound potatoes, peeled and thinly sliced*
- *1 tablespoon butter*
- *1 tablespoon oil*
- *2 slices bacon, diced*
- *1 clove garlic, crushed*
- *1 teaspoon salt*
  Freshly ground black pepper
  Dash of nutmeg
- *¹⁄₂ cup grated Cheddar cheese*

ʼry the potato slices very
ᴛoroughly. In a heavy skillet,
ᴇat the butter and oil. Add the
ɔtato slices, bacon, garlic, salt,
ɛpper and nutmeg and sauté
ᴠer high heat until the potatoes
ʼe tender. Lower the heat,
ɔver the pan and cook for 15
inutes. Uncover, raise the heat
ᴀd, pressing down on the
ɔtatoes with a spatula, cook
ᴀtil a brown crust forms and
ᴇ potatoes form a pancake.
ᴵde the pancake onto a plate
ᴀd invert back into the skillet
 brown the other side. Remove
ɔm the heat and sprinkle on
ᴇ cheese. Cover the skillet and
ᴵow the cheese to melt. Cut
ᴛo wedges and serve hot.

Oignons glacés

Glazed onions

6 servings

- *18 small white onions, peeled*
- *2 tablespoons butter*
- *1 tablespoon olive oil or vegetable oil*
- *¹⁄₂ teaspoon salt*
  Freshly ground black pepper
- *1 bay leaf*
- *¹⁄₂ cup chicken broth*
- *2 tablespoons white vermouth*
- *2 tablespoons finely chopped parsley*

Cut a cross in the root end of each
onion to prevent center from
falling from the onion. Brown
onions in butter and oil. Season
with salt and pepper. Place
onions with their cooking butter
into a baking dish. Add bay leaf,
chicken broth and vermouth.
Cover and continue cooking in
a 350° oven for 1 hour.
Turn onions every 20 minutes.
Garnish with parsley. Serve hot.

Haricots verts à la crème

Green beans

6 servings

- *2 pounds green beans, cleaned and trimmed or 2 packages frozen whole green beans*
- *2 tablespoons butter*
- *1 cup heavy cream*
- *¹⁄₂ teaspoon salt*
  Dash of white pepper
- *1 teaspoon lemon juice*

Plunge the beans into boiling
salted water and cook uncovered
8 to 10 minutes or until not
quite tender. Drain and rinse
under cold water so they retain
their color. If using frozen beans,
cook according to the package
directions. Just before serving,
melt the butter in a large skillet,
add the beans and toss over high
heat for a few minutes. Add the
cream, salt and pepper and bring
to a boil. Cook for about
5 minutes until the cream is
reduced slightly and the beans
are tender. Season with lemon
juice to taste and serve hot.

Tomates farcies à la Niçoise

Stuffed tomatoes Riviera style

4 servings

- *4 medium sized tomatoes*
- *¹⁄₄ pound minced beef, cooked and cooled*
- *1 medium sized onion, finely chopped*
- *1 clove garlic, crushed*
- *1 medium sized potato, cooked and mashed*
- *1 tablespoon finely chopped parsley*
- *¹⁄₄ teaspoon salt*
  Freshly ground black pepper
- *1 egg, lightly beaten*
- *1 tablespoon olive oil or salad oil*
- *¹⁄₄ cup fine breadcrumbs*
- *2 tablespoons butter*

Slice the top off each tomato
and scoop out the pulp with a
teaspoon. Place tomato pulp,
beef, onion, garlic, potato,
parsley, salt and pepper in a
bowl. Combine with the egg and
olive oil. Fill mixture into
tomatoes. Sprinkle each with
breadcrumbs and top with a
pat of butter. Bake in a buttered
baking dish in a 350° oven for
20 minutes. Serve hot.

Ratatouille,
recipe page 70, 3rd column

Champignons Cévenols

Mushrooms provençale

4 servings

 1 pound mushrooms
 ½ cup olive oil
 ¼ teaspoon salt
 1 small clove garlic, crushed
 1 tablespoon finely chopped
   parsley
 4 tablespoons fresh breadcrumbs

Wash the mushrooms. Separate the stems from the caps. Chop the stems finely. In a heavy skillet, heat the oil. Add the caps, cover with a circle of wax paper and cook over low heat 10 minutes. With a slotted spoon, transfer them to a plate or shallow bowl. Add the stems to the skillet, raise the heat and sauté 3 to 4 minutes. With the slotted spoon, remove the stems to a small mixing bowl and mix in the salt, garlic and parsley. Place the mixture on top of the caps. Add the breadcrumbs to the skillet and sauté until golden. Sprinkle over the mushrooms. Cover the plate and let the mushrooms stand 1 day before serving.

Cèpes sautés paysanne

Sautéed mushrooms country style

4–6 servings

 6 slices bacon
 2 pounds cépes or mushrooms
 1 teaspoon lemon juice
 1 small onion, finely chopped
 1 clove garlic, crushed
 2 tablespoons fine dry
   breadcrumbs
 ½ teaspoon salt
   Freshly ground black pepper
 1 tablespoon finely chopped
   parsley

In a large skillet, cook the bacon over low heat until crisp. Drain and crumble. In the pan in which the bacon was cooked, sauté the mushrooms for 3 minutes in the remaining fat. Adding a little butter if necessary. Sprinkle with lemon juice. Add the onion, garlic and breadcrumbs, and sauté over high heat, stirring constantly, for 3 minutes. Add the bacon, salt, pepper and parsley and mix well. Serve hot.
Note: Cépes are one of the many types of mushrooms found in France, Italy and Germany. They are available here both dried and in cans. If you are unable to find any, use fresh mushrooms for this dish. Serve with roast beef.

Large brown cèpes (a kind of mushroom) grow in the extensive pinewood forest located near the city of Bordeaux. On Sundays whole families leave Bordeaux with baskets and pick their way among the trees to look for them.

Cèpes sautés paysanne

Asperges au jambon

Asparagus with ham

6 servings

   2 pounds fresh asparagus
½ teaspoon salt
   2 tablespoons lemon juice
   6 thin slices boiled ham
      Hollandaise sauce (page 26)

Peel lower third of asparagus spears with a potato peeler. Place asparagus in a large skillet. Cover with cold water. Add salt and lemon juice. Simmer uncovered 10 minutes until tender. Place a piece of ham on each individual serving dish. Cover with drained asparagus and spoon Hollandaise sauce over asparagus. Serve immediately.

The large orange pumpkin ripens at the same time as the grapes and always grows along the edges of the vineyard. Soup made from this pumpkin is a traditional dish served to grape-pickers.

Carrotes Vichy

Potiron au gratin

Endives au lard gratinées

Champignons à la Bordelaise

Glazed carrots

6 servings

12 carrots, sliced
½ teaspoon salt
1 tablespoon butter
1 teaspoon sugar
3 tablespoons white vermouth
2 tablespoons finely chopped parsley

Cover carrots with salted boiling water in a skillet. Cover and simmer 15 minutes until almost tender. Drain carrots and return them to the skillet. Add butter, sugar and vermouth. Cook uncovered for 5 minutes until the wine has evaporated and the carrots are glazed and shiny. Garnish with parsley. Serve hot.

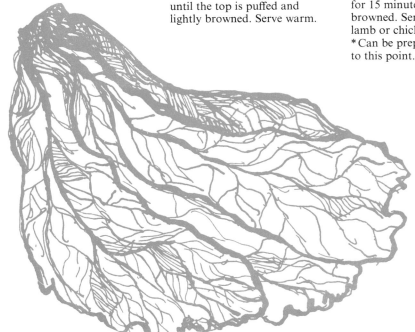

Pumpkin au gratin

4 to 6 servings

1 can (1 pound) pumpkin
½ teaspoon salt
   Freshly ground black pepper
   Dash of nutmeg
¼ teaspoon ground cloves
2 tablespoons melted butter
1 egg
½ cup heavy cream
2 tablespoons grated Parmesan cheese

Thoroughly combine the pumpkin, salt, pepper, nutmeg, cloves and butter. Place in a small, lightly buttered casserole. Beat the egg lightly and mix in the cream and Parmesan cheese. Pour over the pumpkin. Bake in a 400° oven 30 minutes or until the top is puffed and lightly browned. Serve warm.

Endives au gratin

4 servings

8 endives
4 slices bacon
1 tablespoon butter
2 cups Béchamel sauce (see page 26)
½ cup Parmesan cheese, grated

Cut a V-shaped notch in the base of each endive and wash carefully. Simmer whole endives in salted water for 20 minutes. Fry bacon until almost crisp and all the fat has rendered. Cut each bacon slice in half across the width. Wrap each endive in bacon. Place in a buttered baking dish.* Spoon sauce over the endives. Top with cheese and bake in a 375° oven for 15 minutes until lightly browned. Serve hot with roast lamb or chicken.
*Can be prepared in advance to this point.

Stuffed mushrooms

4 servings

1 pound fresh mushrooms
2 tablespoons butter
2 tablespoons olive oil or vegetable oil
4 scallions, finely chopped
2 cloves garlic, crushed
3 tablespoons parsley, finely chopped
¼ teaspoon salt
   Freshly ground black pepp
2 tablespoons lemon juice
¼ cup heavy cream
¼ cup fine breadcrumbs

Wash mushrooms quickly und cold running water and pat th dry on paper towels. Remove the stems from the caps. Saute mushroom caps in hot butter for two minutes on each side until lightly browned. Place ca in a buttered baking dish, hollow side up. Add oil to the skillet. Chop mushroom stems finely. Combine with scallions garlic and parsley. Season wit salt and pepper. Sauté mushr mixture in hot oil and butter five minutes.
Add lemon juice and cream. Simmer five more minutes. Fill this mixture into mushro caps and top with breadcrum Bake 5 minutes in a 400° over just before serving. Serve hot on freshly made toast.

Desserts

Gâteau au chocolat

Generon

In France, very thin, light pancakes are called 'crêpes'. These pancakes originally come from Brittany, where they are still a kind of national dish. In all the small villages and towns of this picturesque province one can find 'crêperies', small restaurants which specialize in these delicious pancakes.
Old Breton women, sometimes still wearing the traditional square white caps, stand behind the stove and manipulate these delicate treats. Crêpes are eaten with all kinds of fillings, both hearty and sweet: with ham, meat or shrimp, and with honey and fruit. In the crêperies of Brittany crêpes are almost always accompanied by cider, the light, sparkling apple wine of the region. The most famous crêpes in France are the 'crêpes Suzette', known all over the world as a very special dessert. According to tradition crêpes Suzette were created some time during the last century by the owner of a small restaurant in Paris located near the Comédie Francaise theater. He is supposed to have gained the inspiration from a very successful play in which the maid, called Suzette, appeared carrying a tray of crêpes. To amuse his theatergoing customers, the owner of the restaurant prepared pancakes drenched in orange liqueur, which he called crêpes Suzette. The recipe caught on and the crêpes Suzette, in all its variations, has become one of the world's best known desserts.

Chocolate cake

8 servings

Cake:
    4 eggs
    ¾ cup sugar
    3 squares (3 ounces) baking
       chocolate
    ¾ cup sifted all purpose flour

Butter Cream:
    ½ cup sugar
    ½ cup water
    8 tablespoons unsalted butter
    3 egg yolks

Decoration:
    ½ cup apricot preserves,
       melted and strained
    6 ounces dark sweet chocolate

Butter and flour a 9 inch cake tin. Beat together the eggs and sugar until they are very thick. Break chocolate into pieces and put on a plate. Put plate on top of a saucepan of simmering water. Cover with another plate and allow the chocolate to melt. Fold ⅓ of the flour and ⅓ of the chocolate into the eggs and sugar. Continue alternating the flour and chocolate until well combined. Place in the prepared cake tin. Bake in a 350° oven for 45 minutes. Unmold and allow the cake to cool. Split the cake (horizontally) into 2 layers. Place sugar and water in a small saucepan. Boil 3 minutes until a thick syrup is formed (238° on a candy thermometer). Beat the egg yolks until thick. Continue beating the eggs while adding hot syrup in a slow

steady stream. Beat 5 more minutes until very thick and doubled in bulk. Beat the butter until softened and lightened in color. Add butter to the egg yolks and syrup, a little at a time. Sandwich butter cream between 2 cake layers. Melt sweet chocolate between two plates set over a saucepan of simmering water. Line a cookie sheet with wax paper. Spread melted chocolate in a very thin layer on the wax paper. Chill chocolate 30 minutes. Brush the top and sides of the cake with the warm, clear liquid from the strained apricot preserves. Crumple the wax paper to break the chocolate into small thin wafers. Scatter chocolate wafers over the top and sides of the cake.

Apple pudding

4 servings

    4 medium sized cooking apples,
       peeled, cored and sliced
    4 tablespoons sugar
    ½ teaspoon cinnamon
    2 tablespoons brandy (optional)
    6 tablespoons butter
    ½ cup sugar
    3 eggs, lightly beaten
    1 teaspoon vanilla
    1 cup flour
    ½ teaspoon baking powder
    2 tablespoons icing
       sugar

Place apples in a 9 inch deep pie dish or 1 quart bowl. Sprinkle with sugar, cinnamon and brandy. Let the apples stand for 1 hour. Beat together the butter and sugar. Add eggs and vanilla and beat for 2 minutes. Fold in the flour and baking powder. Spoon this mixture over the apples and bake in a 375° oven for 35 minutes. Dust with icing sugar. Serve hot with ice cream or sweetened whipped cream.

Gâteau aux raisins

Grape cake

8 servings

2 cups water
8 tablespoons butter cut into
  small pieces
½ teaspoon salt
2 tablespoons sugar
2 cups all purpose flour
8 eggs

Filling:
1 cup sugar
5 egg yolks
¾ cup flour
1 cup milk, simmering
1 cup heavy cream, simmering
1 teaspoon vanilla extract
1 small bunch white grapes
1 small bunch black grapes

Place water, butter, salt and
sugar in a heavy saucepan.
Adjust the heat so that the butter
has completely melted when the
water boils. Remove the pan
from the heat as soon as the
water boils. Add the flour all
at once and stir vigorously.
Return the pan to a moderate
heat for two minutes until the
dough can be formed into a ball.
Remove the pan from the heat
and add the eggs one at a time.
Beat each egg well into the
mixture before adding the next
egg. Butter and flour three
cookie sheets and draw three
9 inch circles in the flour using
a plate as a guide. Spread the
mixture within the circles as
smoothly as possible. Bake 20
minutes in a 350 degree oven.
Turn the oven off and leave
the layers in the oven for another
five minutes. Remove and allow

the layers to cool. In the meantime, prepare the custard. Beat the sugar and eggs together until thick and lemon colored. Beat in the flour. Stir in the combined simmering milk and cream. Place in a saucepan over moderate heat and stir continuously with a wire whisk to form a thick custard. Add the vanilla and cool the custard. To assemble the cake, place one third of the firm, cool custard on the bottom layer and cover with a layer of white and black grapes. Continue with the second layer and arrange the grapes attractively on the top layer. Allow the cake to stand for 1 hour before cutting.

Kougelhopf

Gâteau Saint-Honoré

Tourte au fromage

Millar

Raisin cake

10 to 12 servings

> 1 cup butter
> 5 eggs
> 2⅓ cups all purpose flour, sifted
> ½ teaspoon salt
> 2 tablespoons sugar
> 2 tablespoons lukewarm water
> 1 package dry yeast
> 1 teaspoon vanilla
> 1 teaspoon lemon extract
> 1 cup raisins
> ½ cup slivered almonds
> 2 tablespoons icing sugar

Beat the butter in a bowl until light and fluffy. Add the eggs one at a time and beat well. Add the flour, salt and sugar, beating constantly. Dissolve the yeast in the water and beat into the dough along with the vanilla and lemon extract. Stir in the raisins. Butter a 10″ tube pan and sprinkle the bottom with the almonds. Turn the dough into the pan, distributing it evenly. Cover and let rise until the dough almost reaches the top of the pan. Bake in a 350° oven for 45 minutes. Let the kougelhof cool in the pan for 20 minutes. Turn it out and sprinkle the top with icing sugar. Cool thoroughly before slicing.

Gateau Saint-Honoré

8 servings

Cream puff base:
> 1 cup water
> ¼ teaspoon salt
> 3 tablespoons sugar
> 4 tablespoons butter
> 1 cup sifted all purpose flour
> 4 eggs

Filling:
> 1½ cups heavy cream
> 2 tablespoons sugar
> 1 teaspoon vanilla
> ½ cup apricot preserves, heated and strained
> ½ cup sliced almonds

Decoration:
> 3 tablespoons icing sugar

Prepare the cream puff base following the directions in the recipe for Gougère (page 14). Using two spoons, form the mixture into a 9 inch circle. Bake on a buttered and floured baking sheet in a 375° oven for 30 minutes. Remove from the oven. Cool and cut in half horizontally. Whip the cream until it is slightly thickened. Add the sugar and vanilla. Sandwich cream between the 2 layers of the gateau. Spread the almonds on a baking sheet. Toast almonds in a 350° oven for 8 minutes. Cool the almonds. Brush the top layer of the gateau with clear warm liquid from the strained apricot preserves. Sprinkle with toasted almonds. Dust with sifted icing sugar.

Cheese cake

6 to 8 servings

> 2 egg yolks
> 1½ cups sugar
> 1 package (8 ounce) Philadelphia cream cheese, softened
> ½ cup butter, softened
>   Grated rind of one lemon
> 1 teaspoon vanilla
> 1 cup sifted self-rising flour
> 3 egg whites, stiffly beaten
> 1 pint strawberries
> 1 tablespoon Grand Marnier or other orange liqueur

Beat the egg yolks until they thicken slightly. Add ½ cup of sugar and beat until thick and lemon colored. Add the cream cheese and butter alternately with the remaining sugar, beating constantly. Beat in the lemon rind and vanilla. Fold in the flour carefully until just combined. Stir in ⅓ of the egg whites and fold in the remainder. Place the batter in a well buttered and floured 8 inch spring form cake pan. Tap the pan on the counter a few times to settle the batter. Bake in a 350° oven for 1 hour or until the cake tests done. Let cool in the pan 15 minutes before removing to cool further on a wire rack. Slice the strawberries and sprinkle with Grand Marnier. When ready to serve, place the cake upside down on a serving platter and top with the strawberries.

Corn cake

6 servings

> 1 teaspoon butter
> 1 tablespoon flour
> 1¼ cups sugar
> 5 egg yolks
> ¾ cup sifted all purpose flour
> 2 cups milk, simmering
> 1 (12 ounce) can sweet corn
>   Rind from 1 orange, finely grated
>   Rind from 1 lemon, finely grated
> 1 teaspoon vanilla
> 5 egg whites

Butter and flour a 1½ quart soufflé dish or 9 inch cake tin. Beat 1¼ cups sugar and the egg yolks until very thick. Beat in the flour. Stir in simmering milk. Place in saucepan and heat until thickened into a custard. Add corn and grated orange rind, lemon rind and vanilla. Beat egg whites until they stand in soft peaks. Fold custard into egg whites. Place in the prepared dish and bake in a 375° oven for 25 minutes. Serve immediately.

Fraises Romanoff

Strawberries Romanoff

4 servings

1 (1 quart) box strawberries
3 tablespoons sugar
2 large oranges
2 tablespoons Grand Marnier
1 tablespoon brandy

Remove the stems from the
strawberries and rinse quickly
under cold water. Dry the
strawberries on paper towels.
Place in a serving dish and
sprinkle with sugar. Peel the
oranges. Cut into segments
cutting between the membranes.
Add orange segments to
strawberries. Squeeze orange
juice from remaining pulp over
the strawberries. Add Grand
Marnier and brandy.

Ananas flambé

Pineapple flambéed in Kirsch

4 servings

1 small fresh pineapple
   or 1 (1 pound 14 ounce) can
   pineapple rings, drained
3 tablespoons butter
4 tablespoons sugar
¼ cup Kirsch, warmed
4 scoops vanilla ice cream

Trim pineapple and cut into
8 rings. Melt the butter in a
large skillet. Add pineapple.
Sprinkle with half of the sugar
and cook over high heat until
lightly browned. Turn pineapple
on to the second side, sprinkle
with remaining sugar and
continue cooking until lightly
browned. Add Kirsch and light
with a match. When the flames
have died down, serve hot
pineapple on a scoop of ice
cream in individual serving dishes.
Pour pan juices over the
pineapple.

Moka gâteau

Coffee flavored cake

8 servings

1 cup sifted all purpose flour
¼ teaspoon salt
4 eggs
¾ cup sugar
1 teaspoon instant coffee
⅔ cup ground almonds
   with skins
½ cup apricot preserves
1 cup heavy cream
2 tablespoons sugar
1 teaspoon instant coffee
1 can (1 pound 14 ounces)
   apricot halves, drained
½ cup ground toasted almonds

Butter and flour a 9 inch cake
pan. Line the bottom with a
circle of buttered wax paper.
Sift the flour with the salt.
Beat the eggs with the sugar
and instant coffee until very
thick. Carefully fold in the flour
and ground almonds. Do not
overmix. Place the batter in
the prepared cake pan and
bake in a 375° oven 20 to 25
minutes or until a cake tester
comes out clean. Cool the cake
in the pan for 5 minutes and
then turn out on a wire rack.
Heat the preserves in a small
saucepan and force through
a sieve. Beat the cream until
slightly thickened. Add the sugar
and instant coffee and continue
beating until thick. Split the
cake in half. Spread one cut
side with whipped cream.
Top with the other half, cut
side down. Brush the top and
sides of the cake with strained
apricot glaze. Arrange the
drained apricots on top and brush
them with the glaze. Press the
ground nuts around the sides
of the cake and sprinkle some
on top.

Vacherin aux fraises

Strawberry meringue

10 servings

```
  6  egg whites
 1/8 teaspoon cream of tartar
  1  teaspoon salt
  1  teaspoon vanilla
1 1/2 cups castor sugar
  1  quart vanilla ice cream
 1/2 pound strawberries
 1/2 cup red currant jelly, melted
```

Butter and flour 4 cookie sheets
or cover each with a sheet of
parchment paper. Outline
4–7 inch circles using a plate as
a guide. Place egg whites, cream
of tartar, salt and vanilla in a
large mixing bowl. Beat until
egg whites stand in soft peaks.
Add sugar a spoonful at a time.
Continue beating until egg
whites are stiff. Spoon egg
whites into a large pastry bag
fitted with a No. 5 star tube.
Outline 3 circles with egg whites.
Outline fourth circle in the
same way but fill in the circle
completely with inward radiating
rings of egg white. Reserve
remaining egg whites. Bake
meringues in a 200° oven for
1 hour. Without opening the
oven door, turn oven off and
leave meringues to dry for
1 hour more. Remove meringues
from the oven. On a clean,
buttered and floured cookie
sheet, place rings on top of each
other using remaining meringue
to hold circles in place. Decorate
outside of meringue case with
rosettes of meringue. Return
meringue case to a 200° oven
and bake for 1 hour. Turn oven
off and leave meringue for 1

hour more until it has dried
completely. Fill meringue case
with ice cream and a few sliced
strawberries. Arrange remaining
strawberries on top of the ice
cream and brush with melted
red currant jelly.
The meringue shell can be
prepared 3 or 4 days in advance
and the dessert assembled
just before serving.

Bûche de Noël

Christmas log

10 servings

Batter:
- *8 eggs*
- *1 cup sugar*
- *1 cup ground blanched almonds*
- *1 cup all purpose flour*

Syrup:
- *1 cup water*
- *1 cup sugar*
- *2 tablespoons Kirsch*

Cream:
- *4 egg yolks*
- *1 cup sugar*
- *¼ cup water*
- *1 cup butter, creamed*
- *3 ounces unsweetened redi-blend chocolate*

Decoration:
- *Icing sugar*

Beat the eggs and sugar together until very thick and mousse-like. The mixture will at least triple in volume. Carefully fold in the almonds and flour. Oil a Swiss roll pan, 15½ × 10½ × 1. Line it with a sheet of wax paper longer than the pan. Oil the paper. Turn the batter into the pan and spread it evenly. Bake in a 350° oven 20 to 25 minutes or until it tests done. Meanwhile, combine the sugar and water for the syrup and boil until the sugar is dissolved. Cool completely and add the Kirsch. Place 2 overlapping sheets of wax paper on a board and dust them with icing sugar. Invert the cake on the paper and peel off the wax paper on which the cake was baked. When the cake is cool, brush on the syrup. Add a little at a time until all the syrup is used. Beat the egg yolks in a bowl until thick and creamy. Boil the sugar and ¼ cup water together until the mixture reaches 235° on a candy thermometer or a soft ball forms when a few drops are put into cold water. Beating constantly, pour the hot syrup into the egg yolks in a thin, steady stream. Continue beating a few minutes. Beat in the creamed butter. Reserve 2 tablespoons of the butter cream and beat the chocolate into the remainder. Spread the cake with a thin layer of chocolate buttercream. Beginning at one long edge, roll the cake up onto a long board or serving plate using the wax paper as an aid. Round off the ends and spread them with the white buttercream. Spread the top and sides of the log with the remaining chocolate buttercream. Run the tines of a fork over the buttercream to resemble bark. Sift on a little powdered sugar. Decorate the log with marzipan holly leaves and candied cherries.

Biscuits aux framboises

Raspberry cake

8 servings

- *4 egg yolks*
- *4 egg whites*
- *¾ cup sugar*
- *¾ cup sifted all purpose flour*
- *¼ cup butter, melted*
- *1 teaspoon vanilla extract*

Filling:
- *½ cup sugar*
- *⅓ cup water*
- *3 egg yolks*
- *8 tablespoons butter, softened*
- *2 tablespoons seedless black raspberry preserves*

Decoration:
- *½ cup black raspberry preserves*
- *1 package (1 tablespoon) unflavored gelatin*
- *¼ cup cold water*
- *½ cup sliced almonds, chopped finely*

Beat together the egg yolks and sugar until very thick. Fold in the flour and the melted butter, adding a little of each at a time and folding the mixture over and over. Beat the egg whites until they stand in soft peaks. Fold egg whites into the egg yolk mixture. Pour into a buttered and floured 8 inch cake pan. Bake in a 300° oven for 25 minutes until golden brown and lightly puffed. Remove the cake from the oven and allow it to cool. Split the cake into three layers. In the meantime, prepare the filling. Dissolve the sugar in the water. Place over high heat and boil until syrupy. (238 degrees on a sweet thermometer.) Beat the egg yolks until thick. Continue beating while adding the boiling syrup slowly, in a steady stream of droplets. Continue beating until the mixture is thick. Beat the butter until softened. Beat the butter into the egg yolk mixture. Stir in the raspberry preserves. For the decoration: Sprinkle gelatin on the water and allow to stand undisturbed for five minutes. Heat the preserves and add the gelatin. Simmer until gelatin has dissolved. Allow the preserves to cool. Spread the bottom layer of the cake with most of the butter cream. Stack on the second layer and spread with the cooled jelly. Top with the third layer and spread with the rest of the cream. Spread the sides with the remaining jelly. Press chopped nuts around the sides of the cake. Cut into thin slices for serving.

Cerises à l'eau de vie

Cherries in brandy

3 pounds slightly unripe cherries
4 cups (1 quart) brandy
2 cups sugar
¼ cup water

Remove the stems from the
cherries. Put the cherries in glass
jars. Pour in the brandy. Put the
lids on the jars and leave for
6 weeks in a warm, preferably
sunny, place. Pour the brandy
from the cherries into a jug.
Combine sugar and water and
boil uncovered for 5 minutes.
Cool the syrup and add to the
brandy. Pour back over the
cherries. Close the jars again
and place in a warm place for
14 days before serving. Serve
with ice cream.

Moka parfait

Bavarian coffee-cream

4 servings

1¼ cups milk
½ cup whole dark roast coffee
beans or 1½ teaspoons
instant coffee
3 egg yolks
⅓ cup sugar
⅓ cup water
1 package unflavored gelatin
1 teaspoon sugar
1 tablespoon Kahlua or other
coffee liquer
1 cup heavy cream, partially
whipped
Grated sweet chocolate

Scald the milk with the coffee
beans. Beat the egg yolks with
the sugar until very thick and
mousse-like. Strain the milk
and beat into the egg yolks.
Return the mixture to the pan
and cook, stirring constantly,
over low heat until the mixture
thickens. Allow the mixture to
cool for 10 minutes. Sprinkle the
gelatin over the water to soften.
Add 1 teaspoon sugar and place
over gentle heat, stirring to
melt the gelatin. Add the gelatin
and Kahlua to the cooled egg
mixture. Fold in the cream.
Pour into small individual molds
and refrigerate at least 3 hours.
Decorate with grated sweet
chocolate before serving.

Riz à l'impératrice

Empress rice

8 servings

¾ cup diced candied fruits
4 tablespoons Kirsch
2 cups milk
1 vanilla bean, split or 1
teaspoon vanilla extract
½ cup uncooked rice
½ cup sugar
½ cup dried apricots, cooked
for 30 minutes then drained
1 package unflavored gelatin
¼ cup water
1 teaspoon sugar
½ cup red currant jelly
1¼ cups heavy cream, partially
whipped

Combine the candied fruits and
Kirsch in a small bowl and let
stand while preparing the rice.
In a large saucepan, bring the
milk to a simmer with the vanilla
bean. Add the rice, stir and
simmer slowly until the rice is
tender. Remove from the heat,
discard the vanilla bean or add
vanilla extract if bean was not
used. Stir in the sugar. Add the
marinated fruits. Purée the
apricots in a blender and force
through a sieve to remove the
skins. Add to the rice. Sprinkle
the gelatin over the water to
soften. Add the 1 teaspoon sugar
and place over gentle heat,
stirring to melt the gelatin. Add it
to the rice and mix well. Set in
the refrigerator to cool, stirring
every 15 minutes to suspend the
fruits in the mixture. Oil a 1½
quart mold and place a circle
of wax paper on the bottom.
Melt the red currant jelly and
pour into the mold. Place in the
freezer a few minutes to set the
jelly. When the rice mixture has
started to set slightly, fold in
the cream and turn the mixture
into the mold. Cover with a
circle of oiled wax paper and
refrigerate overnight. Run a knife
around the edge of the mold
and invert the rice on a serving
plate.

Fouasse

Sweet bread

  1 *package dry yeast*
 ¼ *cup lukewarm water*
  1 *cup milk*
  1 *egg*
 ½ *cup sugar*
 ½ *teaspoon cinnamon*
  1 *teaspoon salt*
  6 *tablespoons melted butter*
4 to 4½ *cups all purpose flour*

In a small bowl, sprinkle the yeast over the water. Stir to dissolve. Heat the milk to lukewarm. In a large bowl, combine the egg, sugar, cinnamon and salt, beating until well combined. Add the yeast, milk and 4 tablespoons of the butter and beat again. Stir in the flour gradually until the dough can be gathered into a soft ball. Blend in the remaining flour with your fingers. Turn the dough out onto a lightly floured board and knead until smooth and elastic. The dough will be soft. To prevent sticking, rub your hands occasionally with some of the remaining butter but do not add more flour. Place the dough in a lightly oiled bowl, cover and let rise in a warm place until doubled. Punch the dough down and knead a few times. Divide it into 3 pieces and roll each piece between your hands into a long rope. Braid the ropes, pinching the ends together. Form the braid into a ring and place on an oiled baking sheet. Cover and let rise again until double. Bake in a 350° oven for 35 to 40 minutes.

Tarte aux pommes Normande

Normandy style apple pie

6 servings

  9 *inch unbaked pastry shell*
     (use 1 package frozen pastry,
     thawed and rolled into
     a circle, or pastry recipe
     on page 93) or 1 prepared
     unbaked pie shell
  4 *cups prepared applesauce*
 ⅓ *cup sugar*
  2 *tablespoons apple jack,*
     apple brandy or brandy,
     (optional)
  1 *package unflavored gelatin*
  3 *cooking apples, peeled, cored*
     and sliced thinly
  3 *tablespoons sugar*
  1 *tablespoon lemon juice*
  1 *tablespoon butter*
 ½ *cup apricot preserves, heated*
     and strained
  1 *cup heavy cream*
  2 *tablespoons sugar*
  1 *teaspoon vanilla extract*

Fit pastry into a 9 inch pie plate. Prick with a fork and bake in a 400° oven for 15 minutes. Place applesauce, sugar and brandy in a small skillet. Cook over moderate heat for 15 minutes until thick. Stir to prevent applesauce from sticking to the pan. Place ⅓ cup cold water in a saucepan. Sprinkle gelatin on the water. Allow it to stand undisturbed for 5 minutes. Place pan over low heat until gelatin has dissolved. Stir gelatin into applesauce and then fill into pastry shell. Cover applesauce with apple slices. Sprinkle with sugar and lemon juice and dot with butter. Bake in a 375° oven for 30 minutes.

Brush apples with clear warm liquid from strained apricot preserves. Chill for 4 hours before serving. Whip the cream until it is slightly thickened. Add the sugar and vanilla. Continue beating until very thick. Serve apple pie and whipped cream separately.

Pavé aux marrons

Chestnut block

6 servings

 ¾ *cup sugar*
  3 *tablespoons water*
 ¼ *cup softened butter*
  1 *cup canned unsweetened*
     chestnut purée

For the frosting:
  2 *squares unsweetened chocola*
1½ *tablespoons sugar*
  3 *tablespoons water*
 ¼ *cup butter*

In a small pan, boil the sugar an water together to make a syrup. Beat the softened butter into the chestnut purée. Stir in the syrup. Oil a small loaf pan and line with a strip of wax paper long enough to hang over the long sides of the pan by 2 inches Pour the chestnut mixture into the pan and freeze until set. To prepare the frosting, combine the chocolate, sugar, water and butter in a small saucepan. Stir over low heat until the chocolate is melted. Cool the frosting until it is of spreading consistency. Remove the chestnut mixture from the refrigerator. Run a knife along the sides of the pan and invert onto a serving plate. Spread the frosting evenly over the top and sides of the block with a spatula. Let the frosting solidify a few minutes. Slice and serve.

Mousse au chocolat

Chocolate mousse

6 servings

¼ *pound bitter or semisweet*
  chocolate
4 *egg yolks*
4 *egg whites*
4 *tablespoons butter, softened*
2 *tablespoons Grand Marnier*

Break chocolate into small pieces
and put on a plate. Cover with
another plate. Put the plates
over a saucepan of simmering
water and leave for 10 minutes
until the chocolate has melted.
Beat the egg yolks in a mixer
until they are very thick. Fold in
the butter, orange liquer and
melted chocolate. Beat the
egg whites until they stand in
soft peaks. Fold chocolate
mixture into the egg whites with
a wooden spoon. Divide mixture
between six small dishes. Chill
four hours before serving.

Crêpes Suzettes

Crêpes suzettes

9 servings
18 crêpes

Batter:
1¼ *cups milk*
1 *egg*
1 *egg yolk*
1 *tablespoon butter, melted*
¼ *teaspoon salt*
2 *tablespoons sugar*
1 *cup sifted all purpose flour*
1 *tablespoon vegetable oil*

Sauce:
3 *tablespoons butter*
3 *tablespoons sugar*
  Rind of one orange
  Juice of two oranges
2 *tablespoons Grand Marnier or*
  other orange liquer

Place milk, egg, egg yolk, butter,
salt, sugar and flour in a blender.
Blend one minute until smooth.
Oil frying pan and prepare
crêpes following the directions
for crêpes au meil on page 86.
Heat butter in a large skillet.
Stir in sugar, orange rind and
juice. Roll prepared crêpes in
the sauce. Fold each crêpe in
half and then half again. Arrange
crêpes over the surface of the
skillet. Add Grand Marnier.
Light with a match and serve
flaming.

Crêpes aux fraises

Strawberry crêpes

6 servings

1¼ cups milk
1 egg
1 egg yolk
1 tablespoon butter, melted
1 cup flour
¼ teaspoon salt
2 tablespoons sugar
1 (1 pint) box strawberries
    sliced
2 oranges
2 tablespoons sugar
1 tablespoon Grand Marnier
1 tablespoon butter
2 tablespoons icing sugar,
    sifted

Place milk, egg, egg yolk,
butter, flour, salt and sugar in
a blender. Blend one minute until
smooth. Oil a crêpe pan and
and prepare crêpes following
directions for crêpes au miel on
this page. Slice strawberries and
combine with grated orange
rind. Cut oranges into segments,
cutting between membranes.
Add orange segments, sugar
and Grand Marnier to
strawberries. Fill fruit into
crêpes and roll into cigarette
shapes. Place in a buttered baking
dish. Dot surface of the crêpes
with butter and bake 15 minutes
in a 350° oven. Dust with sifted
icing sugar and serve hot with
whipped cream or ice cream.

Crêpes au miel

Crêpes with honey

6 servings

1¼ cups milk
1 egg
1 egg yolk
1 tablespoon butter, melted
¼ teaspoon salt
2 tablespoons sugar
1 cup sifted all purpose flour
    or wheat flour
1 tablespoon vegetable oil
½ cup honey
6 tablespoons butter

Place milk, egg, egg yolk, 4
tablespoons of butter, salt, sugar
and flour in a blender. Blend one
minute until the batter is smooth.
Heat oil in a small (5½ inch
base) frying pan or crêpe pan.
Pour in a spoonful of batter.
Rotate the pan in all directions
to cover the cooking surface
evenly. Tip out any excess batter.
Cook one minute until crêpe is
lightly browned. Turn and brown
on the second side. (Discard
the first crêpe which will be oily).
Place a teaspoon of butter and
honey on each crêpe. Fold and
serve hot.

Crêpes aux pommes

Crêpes with apples

6 servings
12 crêpes

Batter:
1¼ cups milk
1 egg
1 egg yolk
1 tablespoon butter, melted
¼ teaspoon salt
2 tablespoons sugar
1 cup sifted all purpose flour

Filling:
2 tablespoons butter
3 medium sized cooking apples,
    peeled and cored
2 tablespoons sugar
    Rind and juice of 1 lemon
⅛ teaspoon cinnamon
    Dash nutmeg
1 tablespoon butter
3 tablespoons icing sugar
1 cup heavy cream
2 tablespoons sugar
1 teaspoon vanilla

Place all the batter ingredients
in a blender in the order listed.
Blend one minute until smooth.
Prepare crêpes following the
directions for crêpes au miel on
page 86. Slice apples thinly and
cut into small pieces. Fry apples
in 2 tablespoons butter until
slightly softened, adding sugar,
lemon rind and juice, cinnamon
and nutmeg. Fill apples into
crêpes and roll crêpes like a
cigarette. Butter a baking dish.
Place the crêpes in the dish and
dot with remaining butter.
Place in a 350° oven for 10
minutes. Dust crêpes with sifted
confectioners sugar just before
serving. Serve with heavy cream
combined with sugar and vanilla

Poires Belle-Hélène

Soufflé au Grand Marnier

Pear sundaes

6 servings

6 *Anjou pears, peeled and cored*
1 *cup sugar*
2½ *cups water*
1 *tablespoon lemon juice*
1 *vanilla bean or 1 teaspoon*
vanilla extract
1 *pint vanilla ice cream*
½ *cup sliced almonds*

Sauce:
½ *pound sweet or semi-sweet*
chocolate
½ *cup water*
1 *tablespoon cornflour,*
dissolved in 2 tablespoons
cold water
1 *tablespoon butter, softened*

Place sugar, water and lemon juice and vanilla bean in a heavy saucepan. Bring to boiling point and simmer for 5 minutes. Lower the pears into the syrup and poach pears uncovered for 15 minutes. Remove from the heat and allow pears to cool in the syrup. Add vanilla extract if bean was not used. To prepare the sauce: Melt chocolate in the water, stirring until smooth. Stir in cornflour dissolved in cold water and add the butter. To complete the dish: Put the ice cream in a chilled bowl or individual serving dishes. Stand a pear on the ice cream and pour warm chocolate sauce over the pear. Sprinkle with sliced almonds and serve at once.

Grand Marnier soufflé

4 servings

2½ *tablespoons butter*
3 *tablespoons flour*
1 *cup milk*
¼ *cup sugar*
4 *egg yolks*
¼ *cup Grand Marnier*
1 *teaspoon vanilla*
6 *egg whites*
Pinch of salt
⅛ *teaspoon cream of tartar*
3 *tablespoons icing sugar, sifted*

In a heavy saucepan, melt the butter and add the flour. Cook, stirring for 1 to 2 minutes. Add the milk gradually, beating with a wire whisk. Add the sugar and cook several minutes to form a thick sauce. Remove the pan from the heat and beat in the egg yolks one at a time. Add the Grand Marnier and vanilla. Beat the egg whites with the salt and cream of tartar until stiff peaks form. Stir ¼ of the egg whites into the yolk mixture and carefully fold in the remainder. Butter and sugar a 1½ to 2 quart soufflé dish or other straight sided mold. Place the egg mixture in the dish and bake in a 400° oven for 10 minutes. Lower the heat to 350° and bake 20 minutes more or until the soufflé is puffed and golden. Sprinkle with icing sugar and serve immediately.

Clafouti aux pruneaux

Baked plums

6 servings

   1 pound plums
1¼ cups milk
   4 eggs
  ½ cup sugar
   1 teaspoon salt
   1 cup flour
1½ tablespoons butter, melted
  ¼ cup icing sugar

Remove pits from the plums, and place in an 8 cup baking dish. Combine remaining ingredients, except the icing sugar, in a blender. Blend until smooth. Pour batter over the plums and bake 30 minutes in a 350° oven. Dust surface with sifted icing sugar and serve hot.
This desert can be made with cherries, peaches, apples or other fruits in season. It is particularly good served with whipped cream.

Crème caramel

Soufflé au citron

Pêche Melba

Caramel custard

6 servings

For the caramel:
*   2 tablespoons water*
*   ½ cup sugar*

For the custard:
*   2 cups milk, scalded*
*   1 teaspoon vanilla*
*   4 eggs*
*   ¾ cup sugar*

Have 6 small (½ cup) ovenproof molds ready. In a small heavy saucepan, preferably enameled, place the sugar and water. Bring to a boil, swirling the mixture until the sugar dissolves. Cook until the mixture is a deep, golden brown. (Watch carefully so the caramel is not allowed to burn.) Immediately remove the pan from the heat and hold it in a basin of water for 10 seconds to stop the cooking. Pour a layer of caramel into each mold. Add vanilla to the scalded milk. Beat the eggs together with the sugar until well combined. Stirring constantly, strain the warm milk into the eggs. Pour the custard into the molds. Place the molds in a shallow pan and add water to come halfway up the sides of the molds. Place in a 350° oven and bake for 35 minutes or until custard is set. Chill for 2 hours. Run a knife around the inside of each mold and invert the custard on individual dessert plates.

Cold lemon soufflé

8 servings

*   5 eggs*
* 1½ cups sugar*
*   Juice (¾ cup) and grated rind of 3 large lemons*
*   2 packages gelatin*
*   ½ cup water*
*   1 teaspoon sugar*
*   2 cups heavy cream, partially whipped*
*   Pinch of salt*
*   ⅛ teaspoon cream of tartar*
*   ¼ cup macaroon crumbs or toasted ground almonds*
*   ¾ cup heavy cream, whipped*
*   2 tablespoons ground pistachio nuts*

Butter and sugar a 1½ quart soufflé dish or other straight sided mold. Tie a collar of oiled and sugared wax paper or aluminum foil around the mold to extend the sides. (Be sure to oil the collar. Butter will solidify when chilled and the soufflé will stick to the paper.) Separate the eggs and beat the yolks with the sugar and lemon rind, adding the lemon juice gradually, until the mixture is very thick and mousse-like. Do not underbeat. Sprinkle the gelatin over the water to soften. Add 1 teaspoon sugar and stir over low heat to dissolve the gelatin. Cool and add to the lemon mixture, combining thoroughly. Fold in the partially whipped cream. Beat the egg whites with the salt and cream of tartar until stiff peaks form. Fold into the lemon mixture. Turn into the prepared soufflé dish and

chill in the refrigerator until set. Remove the collar and decorate the sides of the soufflé with macaroon crumbs and the top with the whipped cream and pistachio nuts.

Peach Melba

4 servings

*   2 large ripe peaches*
*   1 cup sugar*
*   2 cups water*
*   ½ vanilla bean or 1 teaspoon vanilla extract*
*   1 package frozen raspberries*
*   4 scoops vanilla ice cream*
*   4 tablespoons, sliced almonds, toasted 5 minutes on a cookie sheet in a 350° oven*

Dissolve sugar in water in a small saucepan over low heat. Split vanilla bean in half lengthwise. Scrape inner part into the syrup and add the remaining part. Simmer five minutes. Add whole peaches and simmer five minutes. Drain peaches and remove the skin. Cut each peach in half. Add vanilla extract to syrup if vanilla bean was not used. Allow peaches to cool in the syrup. Thaw raspberries. Drain raspberries and reserve syrup. Force through a strainer. Add ⅓ cup of raspberry syrup to form a thick sauce. Place a scoop of ice cream in 4 serving dishes. Add drained poached peach half. Top with raspberry sauce and scatter each dish with cooled, toasted almonds.

Compôte de pruneaux

This dessert, sublimely simple, was created in 1893 by the famous French chef, Escoffier, who was then head cook at the elegant Savoy in London. He named it in honor of the world-famous Australian opera singer, Nellie Melba.

Plum compôte

4 servings

> 2 pounds plums with pits removed
> ½ cup sugar
> ¼ cup water
> Rind and juice of 1 orange
> ½ cup Port wine or other sweet red wine
> 2 tablespoons red currant jelly
> ½ teaspoon almond extract
> ½ cup sliced almonds

Place all the ingredients except the almond extract and almonds in a saucepan. Cover and simmer over low heat for 20 minutes. Add almond extract. Chill for 4 hours. Sprinkle with sliced almonds just before serving.

Pêches au vin

Peaches in white wine

4 servings

- 4 *large ripe peaches*
- 4 *teaspoons quick dissolving sugar*
- 8 *tablespoons sweet white wine*

Drop the peaches into boiling water for 15 seconds. Drain and rinse them under cold water. Remove the skins and slice each into a large wine glass. Sprinkle each serving with 1 teaspoon sugar and add 2 tablespoons wine. Let stand at least ½ hour before serving.

Choux aux fraises

Cerises flambées

Omelette Normande

Cream puffs with strawberries

8 servings

Pastry base:
1 cup water
4 tablespoons butter, cut into small pieces
¼ teaspoon salt
1 tablespoon sugar
1 cup sifted all purpose flour
4 eggs

Filling:
1 cup sugar
5 egg yolks
¾ cup flour
1 cup milk, simmering
1 cup heavy cream, simmering
1 teaspoon vanilla extract
1 quart strawberries
½ cup red currant jelly, melted

Place water, butter, salt and sugar in a heavy saucepan. Adjust the heat so that the butter has completely melted when the water boils. Remove pan from the heat as soon as the water boils. Add the flour all at once and stir vigorously. Return the pan to a moderate heat for two minutes until the dough can be formed into a ball. Remove the pan from the heat and add the eggs one at a time. Beat each egg well into the mixture before adding the next egg. Butter and flour two cookie sheets. Using 2 spoons form balls of dough about the size of an egg and place 3 inches apart. Bake in a 375° oven for 25 minutes until puffed and golden. In the meantime prepare the filling. Beat the sugar and egg yolks until thick and lemon colored. Beat in the flour. Stir in simmering milk and cream. Place in a saucepan over moderate heat and stir continuously to form a medium thick custard. Cool the custard. It will become thicker as it cools. Slice the top from each cream puff. Fill with cooled custard and top with strawberries. Brush strawberries with melted red currant jelly to make them shine. Decorate plates with remaining strawberries glazed with jelly.

Flambéed cherries

6 servings

1 pound fresh cherries or
1 (1 pound) jar cherries, pitted
½ cup water
1 cup sugar
1 tablespoon arrowroot or cornflour, dissolved in 2 tablespoons cold water
1 teaspoon vanilla extract
1 tablespoon cherry brandy
¼ cup brandy, warmed

Remove stems and pits from fresh cherries. Simmer water and sugar in a saucepan for five minutes. Add cherries and simmer five more minutes. (Or simmer canned cherries in ¾ cup of cherry juice.) Remove cherries with a slotted spoon. Add cornflour paste to syrup and cook one minute until thickened. Remove pan from the heat. Add vanilla and cherry brandy. Pour warmed brandy over cherries. Light with a match and serve flaming cherries with ice cream.
Other fruit can also be flamed in this manner: e.g. apricots flavored with apricot brandy and flamed with kirsch; peaches flavored with peach brandy and flamed with white rum, pears flavored with crème de cacao and flamed with dark rum.

Apple omelette

4 servings

3 small tart apples, peeled, cored and sliced thinly
Juice of one lemon
4 tablespoons butter
2 tablespoons superfine sugar
¼ teaspoon cinnamon
Dash of nutmeg
1 tablespoon apple brandy
6 eggs
3 tablespoons apple brandy, warmed
½ cup heavy cream, whipped and sweetened with 1 tablespoon sugar

Sprinkle the apple slices with lemon juice. Melt 2 tablespoons of the butter in a skillet and sauté the apples until soft. Add 1 tablespoon of the sugar, the cinnamon, nutmeg and 1 tablespoon apple brandy. Keep the mixture warm. Stir the eggs together lightly with a fork. In a 10 inch omelette pan or skillet with rounded sides, melt the remaining butter. When very hot, pour in the eggs and stir vigorously with a fork until partially set. Place the apple mixture on one half of the omelette and fold over the other half. Let the omelette brown for a few seconds and turn out onto a serving dish. Sprinkle with the remaining sugar. Heat a metal skewer until very hot and burn a cross design on the omelette. Ignite the warmed apple brandy, and pour the flames over the omelette. Serve with sweetened whipped cream.

Kitchen terms

'Al dente'
Literally: to the tooth. This term is particularly used for vegetables and pasta which, though tender, have some bite left in them.

Aspic
A stiff gelatine obtained by combining fish or meat bouillon with gelatine powder.

Au gratin
Obtained by covering a dish with a white sauce (usually prepared with grated cheese) and then heating the dish in the oven so that a golden crust forms.

Baste
To moisten meat or other foods while cooking to add flavor and to prevent drying of the surface. The liquid is usually melted fat, meat drippings, fruit juice or sauce.

Blanch (precook)
To preheat in boiling water or steam. (1) Used to inactivate enzymes and shrink food for canning, freezing, and drying. Vegetables are blanched in boiling water or steam, and fruits in boiling fruit juice, syrup, water, or steam. (2) Used to aid in removal of skins from nuts, fruits, and some vegetables.

Blend
To mix thoroughly two or more ingredients.

Bouillon
Brown stock, conveniently made by dissolving a bouillon cube in water.

Broth
Water in which meat, fish or vegetables have been boiled or cooked.

'En papillote'
Meat, fish or vegetables wrapped in grease-proof paper or aluminum foil (usually first sprinkled with oil or butter, herbs and seasonings) and then baked in the oven or grilled over charcoal. Most of the taste and aroma are preserved in this way.

Fold
To combine by using two motions, cutting vertically through the mixture and turning over and over by sliding the implement across the bottom of the mixing bowl with each turn.

Fry
To cook in fat; applied especially (1) to cooking in a small amount of fat, also called sauté or pan-fry; (2) to cooking in a deep layer of fat, also called deep-fat frying.

Gnocchi
Small balls or dumplings usually made from semolina or potatoes.

Marinate
To let food stand in a marinade

usually an oil–acid mixture like French dressing.

Parboil
To boil until partially cooked. The cooking is usually completed by another method.

Poach
To cook in a hot liquid using precautions to retain shape. The temperature used varies with the food.

Polenta
A thick porridge obtained by boiling cornmeal.

Reduce
To concentrate the taste and aroma of a particular liquid or food (e.g. wine, bouillon, soup, sauce etc.) by boiling in a pan with the lid off so that the excess water can evaporate.

Roast
To cook, uncovered, by dry heat. Usually done in an oven, but occasionally in ashes, under coals or on heated stones or metals. The term is usually applied to meats but may refer to other foods such as potatoes, corn and chestnuts.

Sauté
To brown or cook in a small amount of fat. See Fry.

Simmer
To cook in a liquid just below the boiling point, at temperatures of 185°–210°.

Bubbles form slowly and collapse below the surface.

Skim
To take away a layer of fat from soup, sauces, etc.

Stock
The liquid in which meat or fish has been boiled together with herbs and vegetables.

Whip
To beat rapidly to produce expansion, due to incorporation of air as applied to cream, eggs, and gelatine dishes.

Conversion table for oven temperatures

fahrenheit degrees:	oventemperature term:
up to 225°	**Cool**
225–275°	**Warm or very slow**
275–325°	**Slow**
350–375°	**Moderate**
400–450°	**Hot**
450–500°	**Very hot**
500°	**Extremely hot**
higher	

Alphabetical index

Index by type of dish

88 Baked plums
83 Bavarian coffee-cream
90 Caramel custard
78 Cheese cake
83 Cherries in brandy
84 Chestnut block
75 Chocolate cake
85 Chocolate mousse
82 Christmas log
79 Coffee flavored cake
90 Cold lemon soufflé
78 Corn cake
93 Cream puffs with
   strawberries
85 Crêpes suzettes
86 Crêpes with apples
86 Crêpes with honey
83 Empress rice
93 Flambéed cherries
78 Gateau Saint-Honoré
87 Grand Marnier soufflé
76 Grape cake
84 Normandy style apple pie
92 Peaches in white wine
90 Peach Melba
87 Pear sundaes
79 Pineapple flambéed in
   Kirsch
91 Plum compôte
78 Raisin cake
82 Raspberry cake
79 Strawberries Romanoff
86 Strawberry crêpes
80 Strawberry meringue
84 Sweet bread

French

Hors d'oeuvres

19 Artichauts vinaigrette
13 Coquilles St. Jacques
   provençale
16 Crousatade aux fruits de mer
19 Escargots à la
   Bourguignonne
18 Foie de poulet
14 Gougère
18 Oeufs au crevettes
17 Pâté de volaille
12 Pipérade Basquaise
15 Pissaladière
12 Quiche au jambon
18 Quiche Lorraine
14 Salade Niçoise
14 Tarte à l'oignon
17 Terrine de poulet

Soups

23 Elzekaria
22 Garbure
22 Potage crécy
23 Potage de tomates
22 Potage Parmentier
21 Potage paysanne
23 Potage Saint Germain
20 Soupe à l'oignon
22 Soupe au potiron
21 Velouté laitue

Sauces

24 Aioli
29 Bouillon blanc de veau
29 Bouillon blanc de volaille
29 Bouillon brun
29 Bouillon de poisson

28 Mayonaise
25 Sauce Béarnaise
26 Sauce Béchamel
27 Sauce Espagnole
26 Sauce Hollandaise
27 Sauce Madère
27 Sauce Mornay
27 Sauce mousseline
26 Sauce ravigotte
25 Sauce velouté
28 Sauce verte
25 Sauce vinaigrette

Fish dishes

36 Barbue Mornay
30 Bar poché
39 Bouillabaisse
36 Buissons d'éperlans
30 Cotriade
35 Crevettes à la crème
42 Crevettes à l'estragon
36 Grenouilles
35 Homard à l'Armoricaine
42 Maquereaux au fenouil
44 Maquereaux marinés au vin
   blanc
36 Merlan au vin rouge
42 Moules marinière
34 Poisson aux câpres
32 Quenelles de brochet
   Nantua
43 Rougets aux fines herbes
43 Rougets farcis aux
   échalotes
31 Salade de tourteau
39 Saumon diable
31 Saumon poché
32 Sole à la Normande
34 Sole Bercy
34 Sole Deauvilloise
38 Truite farcie
40 Truites aux amandes

Meat dishes

47 Beckenoff
51 Blanquette de veau
50 Boeuf à la Bourguignonne
46 Boeuf à la mode
55 Boeuf aux champignons
49 Cassoulet
48 Choucroute Alsacienne
47 Côte de boeuf à la Bordelaise
52 Côte de veau Vallée d'Auge
56 Côtelettes de mouton
   Comtoise
54 Côtelettes de porc au cidre
50 Entrecôte marchand de vin
45 Estouffade de boeuf
51 Filet de boeuf en croûte
55 Foie de veau Véronique
56 Gigot d'agneau à la
   Bretonne
48 Jambon persillé
56 Navarin de mouton
54 Noisettes de porc aux
   pruneaux
46 Pot au feu
53 Rognons de veau aux
   tomates
55 Selle d'agneau bouquetière
50 Steak au poivre
52 Veau à la Niçoise

Poultry and game dishes

57 Canard aux pruneaux
58 Canard Montmorency
58 Canards à l'orange en gelée
62 Coq au vin
64 Coq au vin blanc
67 Dinde à la Poitevine
59 Pintadeaux farcis
61 Poule au pot
62 Poule au thym
63 Poulet à la Basquaise

Vegetable dishes

Desserts

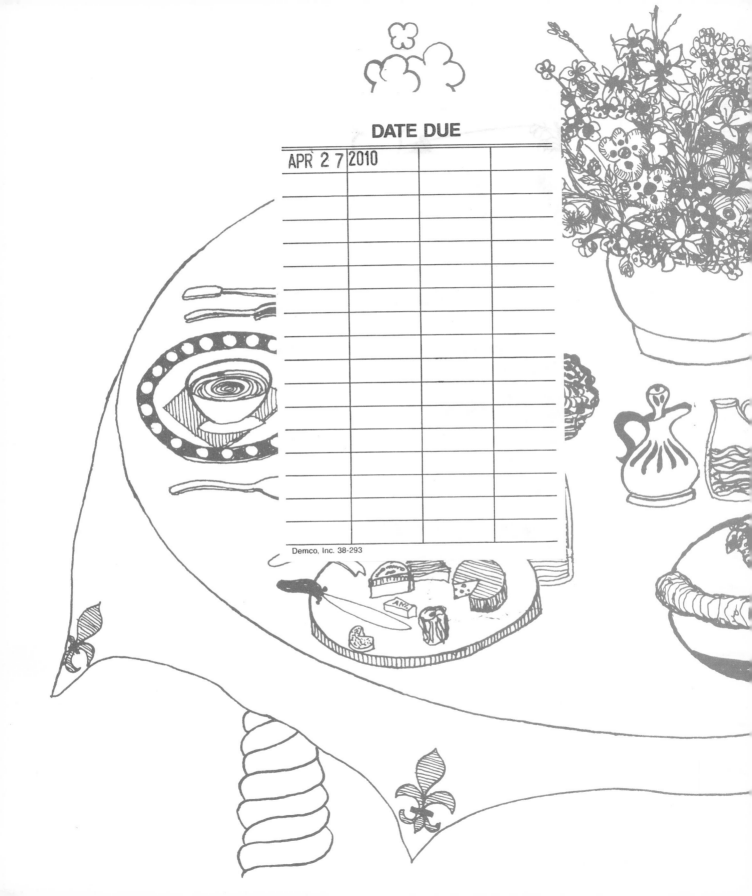

DATE DUE

APR 2 7 2010		